NATIONAL PARKS

NATIONAL PARKS

What happens, in the near future, when Congress plans to bail out a bankrupt America by selling the national parks to the highest bidders

Published by Frogworks Publishing

ROLF MARGENAU

Published in the United States by Frogworks Publishing

ISBN 10 : 0988231182
ISBN—9780988231184
Ebook ISBN—978-0-9882311-9-1
Library of Congress Control Number: 2016905292
Frogworks.com LLC, Lebanon, NJ

www.frogworks.com

First Edition

By Rolf Margenau

PISTILS AND POETRY
PUBLIC INFORMATION
MASTER GARDENER
HIGH ANDES
THE COMMODE COMPANION

DECAPITATED ROSES

The news Grover conveyed through his fob connection to the antique Prius' tinny speakers was so alarming that Portia lost control of the car. Without a lane change corrector or Autobrake® features, the vehicle jumped the curb on the leafy Georgetown street, mowing down a well-tended hedge of azaleas and decapitating ranks of yellow hybrid roses. In panic, she turned the wheel to the right and depressed the brake hard, causing the car to plow four-inch divots into the manicured lawn before it severed the post that supported a nostalgic mailbox reproduction whose sole purpose was to display the name "Hatchett." The mailbox attached itself to the front of the Prius, which now stopped with an ominous cloud of steam arising from beneath the hood. Somehow, the airbag had not deployed.

The Bluetooth system still worked; Grover's voice, now worried and concerned, still carried through the speakers.

"Porrie, Porrie, what the hell is going on? What happened? What's going on? Talk to me!"

"Oh shit, Grover, I just destroyed Senator Hatchett's mailbox."

"You okay?"

"Except for terminal embarrassment and a bump on my chest, I'm fine. And it looks like someone's coming this way."

A large black man holding garden shears looked at Portia with a worried expression. He noted the divots in the lawn, the mailbox perched atop the Prius, the haphazardly strewn roses, and the young woman, pale faced and shaking slightly, tightly gripping the wheel.

He helped her from the car to an iron bench near the entrance to the house. Grover, his voice now transferred to her fob, was still demanding answers, and Portia interrupted to send him her location so he could call a tow truck. He promised to come as soon as he could. The man offered Portia a glass of water and fetched a flexible tablet from the house so she could export insurance information from her fob. Sipping the water, she began to calm down.

Though shaken by the accident, she was more disturbed by Grover's announcement that the House bill to defund and privatize the national parks had left committee and was scheduled to be taken up before the next recess. The artfully drafted bill, he explained, provided that a substantial portion of the proceeds of the sale of the parks would be allocated to projects and causes, including funding for early education, basic scientific research, and infrastructure development, strongly favored by the minority party. There was speculation that there would be enough votes from the minority party to pass the bill.

The so-called "4-H Club" in the Senate, which ironically included Senator Hatchett whose mailbox now rested on the hood of her car, was girding for action. Hatchett and her fellow senators prepared to shepherd the Senate bill to privatize the parks through the steps necessary to require an up-and-down vote.

To Portia Merson, assistant general counsel of the National Green Defense League (NGDL), the prospect of such a cataclysmal legislative event was devastating. She had lobbied a select group of senators and representatives for over a year, using her many talents to explain the folly of selling off the national parks and trading national patrimony for cash. It was an uphill battle. Those members of Congress who had withheld proper funding from the parks for many years saw an opportunity to avoid further nasty confrontations from tree huggers and environmentalists. Sell the parks and be done with it! Let new owners deal with those sticky issues.

Grover, Portia's husband, also explained that commercial interests had drafted numerous "protections" to assure that only American corporations could bid on the parks, that they would remain "pristine" for at least a decade, and would be available to all who completed an Internet application form and paid an appropriate fee. As with any legislation, there were loopholes, about which Portia could only guess. How devastating, she thought, that all her efforts to thwart the legislation seemed to have been for naught. That feeling of inadequacy contributed to her distracted moment when the Prius jumped the curb.

The tow truck, hovering slowly down the street on its air cushion looking for a disabled vehicle, slowed and stopped in front of the senator's home just as a large black Cadalincoln Suburban Attack Vehicle with opaque windows turned the corner and lumbered to a stop in front of the tow truck.

The truck disgorged a friendly looking young man holding a fob, pulling on leather gloves, who strolled toward, Portia, who was still sitting on the bench. The SAV's driver door opened and a stern man with close-cropped hair in a dark blue suit emerged, rushing to the passenger door and opening it with a flourish and a little bow.

A short, stocky woman with hair that was either a lacquered russet wig or the product of a demented hairdresser, stepped from the SUV, adjusted her fashionable gray suit, flounced the bright scarf at her neck, and looked across the front of the property. Her gaze fastened on the ruined lawn, fence, mailbox, and roses. Slowly she walked toward the ruined hedge of roses, bent down to examine the pulpy ends of twigs and the blasted buds, gleaming, scattered on the grass like spent shells after combat. She turned to the man waiting by the passenger door of the SAV.

"Jeez, Brian, look what they did to my friggin' roses," said Senator Deborah Hatchett, senior senator from a well-known state far south of the Mason-Dixon Line, and staunch member of the Senate's 4-H Club.

Turning from the ruined roses, she noted the truck driver speaking with an attractive young woman sitting on the iron bench under the magnolia tree. The senator sniffed the air like a stag in rut and moved toward Portia, cataloging all aspects of the younger woman's appearance—*qualifying* her for future reference. That was the term used when a possible client walked through the door of the real estate brokerage she had operated all those years ago. Before entering politics, she made her fortune as an affordable housing magnate, which the local newspaper unkindly referred to as her "slumlord" business. Nevertheless, the old habit lingered, and she employed her formidable powers of observation and memory to qualify people who crossed her path, for better or worse. The young woman seemed subdued, as well she should be, having trashed her yard with that stupid little car.

The truck driver left to attach a cable to the still slightly steaming car, managing to trample a few of the remaining rose bushes. The young woman turned to the senator, eyes direct, and her body braced for what was probably about to come. She was more handsome than pretty, with wide-set hazel eyes, a generous mouth, a trim nose, and short auburn hair. Tall and slender, she wore a beige business suit with a knee-length skirt. One of her stockings was torn at the calf, and there were smudges of unknown origin on the right side of the skirt. She wore a wedding band and a thin strand of gold at her neck. She was familiar, but Senator Hatchett could not exactly place her.

The senator decided her demeanor was that of a woman accustomed to wielding competent authority—definitely not some low-ranking functionary in a government office. Successful politician that she was, the senator employed well-honed aspects of various personas to fit the occasion. The role of friendly patrician was probably appropriate in this instance.

"You okay, hun?" she asked.

"Frankly, I am a bit shook up, but I will certainly get over it. I am terribly sorry about what happened to your yard, Senator. I promise I will arrange to have everything put back in good order."

"That's just fine, dear. I'm sure Franklin will be able to sort it all out in a day or two. That's why we have insurance, isn't it?"

The senator moved to the bench and sat next to Portia, examining her more closely, taking one hand in hers.

"So you know I am a senator. I do have the strongest feeling that we have met before. Where was it, do you recall?"

Portia had thought about their prior meeting about the same time the Hatchett mailbox left its mooring and bounced onto the hood of her car. She explained.

"Yes, it was at one of the inaugural balls. I don't recall which one, but you were having such a good time, dancing and enjoying the festivities. You seemed very happy and were talking about the inaugural address. Then you slipped where someone had spilled a drink and fell on top of my husband, who was sitting next to me at our table. He is Grover Merson, chief counsel to Congresswoman Pert Pewtree—and I am Portia. We managed to untangle ourselves, and you decided to join us for a nightcap."

"Of course, of course. Portia! You are the lawyer who works for the green something."

They continued chatting amicably, though they represented, respectively, opposite ends of the political spectrum. Portia seethed silently because Senator Hatchett was cosponsor of the legislation designed to privatize the nation's national parks.

As they talked, Portia saw the Selfer® carrying Grover descend onto the street just as the Prius settled onto the back of a flatbed tow truck. It was unnecessary to wave to him; the senator's ruined front yard spoke volumes. He hurried toward the two women, wearing a look of relief as he saw that Portia appeared uninjured and was engaged in conversation with one of the most powerful members of the Senate. As he approached, Senator Hatchett smiled at him and held out her hand, limp at the wrist, as though expecting him to kiss her knuckles. He managed to slip his fingers under the hand and execute an infirm handshake. Her smooth, cool, dry hand reminded him of childhood days when he had been fascinated with garter snakes.

Wylie Cypher settled comfortably in the front section of the sub-orbital Chicago flight, playing blackjack on the big screen in front of him, when his fob buzzed. He intended to ignore it, but changed his mind when the buzz changed to Portia's distinctive chime. He reclined his seat until his head was in the sound chamber, where his conversation would not be overheard, and plugged the detachable Bluetooth button in his ear. Portia's voice was crisp, clear, and urgent.

She had not spoken with her grandfather for a week or so and, following the rules of her upbringing, she did not immediately raise the questions on her mind. Instead she asked how he was. Was he looking forward to the Chicago meetings? Would Linda be joining him. Would he be back in DC soon?

Pleased to be speaking with his favorite grandchild, Wylie responded pleasantly, suspecting this was not a courtesy call, that Portia needed solace, guidance, or simply to vent. He waited.

"Did you hear about the parks?"

"Yes, I received a blast from shit dad's chief a little while ago. Damn shame that Congress sat on its hands for years and bankrupt our country, and now figures it can bolster the economy by spending the proceeds from the sale of our parks. I'm sure it is disappointing for you."

Portia, caught off guard by the reference to "shit dad," searched her memory and recalled that was how her grandfather called the senior senator from Louisiana when they were young men during the Korean War. Wylie, now in his late eighties, occasionally slipped and gave preference to first-learned names and expressions. Just as Portia sorted out her grandfather's slip of the tongue, he added, "I mustn't be so vulgar, darling. Senator Rowe, of course. Unfortunate business, the parks thing. Should we be seriously concerned?"

"I think we should, Wylie. There is a chance the bill will pass the Senate, and no one doubts that President Hofnarr will sign it if he has the chance. Right now I am heartsick!"

Wylie offered soothing words to his granddaughter, saying he would do what he could, although his influence and expertise focused on environmental issues like climate change and misuse of agricultural chemicals. However, privatization of the country's national parks certainly qualified as an environmental issue. He sighed.

Portia clicked off. Wylie looked at his fob to confirm his arrival time and scrawled a reminder on the notepad it projected on the back of the seat in front of him. Sharp green letters appeared; his assistant reminded him of his reservation at Alinea that evening. Linda would meet him there at eight. He smiled and pressed the "massage" button on the armrest. He was eager to see his wife again.

Sneath Naydir used both thumbs to loosen the champagne cork, which reached escape velocity as it rocketed through the foam-paneled ceiling above his desk and lodged in the wiring above, causing the lights in the room to blink madly. Elecbots® scurried from the walls to remedy the damaged wires before Sneath filled the first of the six champagne glasses arrayed on his genuine mahogany sideboard. Three of his partners in their lobbying firm and two assistants surrounded the sideboard, looking forward to feeling expensive bubbles on their tongues. Sneath was fond of the name "Susan," so both his assistants had that first name, distinguished as "Suz" and "Susie." Susie leaned forward to claim her glass of champagne and pointed to a glistening display on his desk.

"Congressman, there's a bunch of congratulations here that I highlighted for you. It's the usual stuff, except for the encrypted message from Boris. It's red-starred, so I can't open it. You'll need your thumbprint to hear what he has to say."

Sneath nodded, accepting the implied reverence from his assistant, and permitted his rotund face to break into a smile. As a former congressman and currently successful Washington lobbyist, he felt justifiably proud to have pried the Parks Act out of committee to the House floor, where it would inevitably be passed. He moved his stocky body closer to their little group and continued passing champagne.

In addition to the Susans, junior partner Bob Robert, the firm's specialist in redundancy, raised his glass to Sneath. Senior partner Felix Roostenberger along with Sneath's best friend and managing partner, Phylander Musti, joined him. They celebrated the successful culmination of long months of lobbying their contacts on the hill and exercising their clients' constitutional rights to spend large amounts of undisclosed funds to influence legislation.

Phylander took a long draught of his champagne, replaced his glass on the sideboard, clasped Sneath's shoulder, and began pounding the sideboard with his other hand, creating a satisfying beat, like a pileated woodpecker deconstructing a hollow tree. In moments, all four men were pounding on the sideboard, a primal exercise that filled the large office with the resounding sound of abused wood, soon followed by orgiastic cries and moans as the men reached back to aboriginal origins to celebrate a great victory. The two women, not previously privileged to observe this ritual of celebration at their K Street lobbying firm, withdrew to a far corner of the office, doing their best to cheer on their superiors.

The rite completed, the three partners, faces flushed and palms sore, drained refilled glasses, congratulated Sneath once more, and returned to their paneled offices, snapping on their fobs, pressing virtual keys on their desktops, preparing to release fresh weapons of mass distraction.

Sneath settled into the genuine leather chair by his desk and began to scroll through the voice messages on his fob, a chorus of congratulations from clients and legislators.

"Sonofagun, you pulled it off, man. We'll finally get some professional management of the parks!"

"Sneath, I never doubted that you and your team could make it happen. Excellent work! We're finally on the path to converting all those underused acres into some real money to address our urgent financial needs."

"Splendid effort, Congressman! You taught those greenicks a lesson they won't forget. Call me soon. We need to discuss ways to convince the BLM [Bureau of Land Management] to reopen logging roads and approve stumpage contracts so we can harvest timber before the pine bark beetle gets there first."

"Sneath, it's Harry. I have some ideas about prioritizing distribution of proceeds from the parks sales. Our bridge division stands ready to ramp up for infrastructure repairs, but we need to minimize the impact of our bridge in Connecticut that collapsed and killed all those people. Give me a ring."

Sneath sighed at Harry's lack of understanding of modern communications. He would have to warn him again about talking about sensitive matters on an unsecure channel (anonymous hackers having recently erased billions of NSA-recorded telephone, Skype, and z-mail threads). And "give me a ring!" Didn't Harry realize how antiquated that phrase was?

He glanced at Frank Crouch's terse message. A major client, the leader of the Crouch Triplets' Crouch Industries, Frank was both generous financially and demanding of his time. His message was simple: "Call me by ten tonight. Keep up the pressure."

The red star communication from Boris popped up and Sneath waved his thumb over the recognition icon. Boris' permanently flushed face immediately appeared on the screen, the details of his plush surroundings contrasting with his craggy features and thornbush tufts of hair. His image paused briefly as the double encryption key hashed and rehashed the digital bits sent earlier from his lair in London. For a moment, Sneath saw a double image of Boris' face, neither particularly flattering.

Boris was a disgraced Russian oligarch who had unwisely challenged President Rockoff, who unseated Putin after his eighteen-year reign. Boris soon faced charges of pederasty and stock swindling and found himself staring at brick walls in prison at Lubyanka Square. He traded a large portion of his fortune for freedom and Rockoff and top members of the Politburo began to enjoy the benefits of ownership in most of Boris' businesses. Boris settled in his sumptuous London penthouse and cast about for new investments. He was naturally drawn to America's national parks.

"Sneath, *boychik*," Boris said, as his face sharpened on Sneath's screen, his rubbery jowls wiggling, his lips shining from his habit of tongue-checking his upper lip every few seconds, "I congratulate you. Even here in London we are, how does it go, agog? Yes, agog. AGOG."

Sneath could tell that Boris was proud that he had learned a new English word, and let him continue with his congratulations. He did so for a few more moments before moving closer to the camera, almost filling the screen with his left eye.

"*Boychik*, you know what I want. It is Grand Canyon. GRAND CANYON."

"Yes, I know. We have discussed that in the past. However, Boris, you know that purchasers must be American citizens. It will be difficult to place you or your business in that category."

"I have big apartment in New York, Central Park. I have *dacha* in Vail. I have condominium in Disney World. I feel like American citizen. You will make it so. And also make sure that *prisoski petukh*, that Frank Crouch, he does not get my Grand Canyon. You be sure about that!"

Sneath discerned a touch of menace in Boris' demand. He assured his client he would do his best.

BEDROOM TALK

"Ow! Owow!" muttered Portia as Grover shifted his body above her. Thinking her outcry meant he was doing something wrong, he rolled aside to the edge of the bed and flicked on the bed stand light, revealing his wife up on her elbows, looking down at her breasts. Even in the low light, he saw the thick blue-black bruise running from her left shoulder to her right thigh, bisecting her breasts, creeping ominously across her left breast toward the nipple.

"I'm sorry," she said. "I didn't mean to cry out. This thing just started to hurt a lot. I...I didn't notice it until just now."

Grover moved closer to his wife to examine the nasty bruise, worried about her, forgetting the abrupt end to lovemaking. Under other circumstances, he would have taken customary pleasure in observing her well-rounded breasts, thin blue veins subtly outlining rusty aureole and crimson nipples, but now he saw the incursion of dark blood, and shuddered at the pain she must be feeling. He caressed her cheek and stroked her dark hair.

"I'm the one who's sorry. Sorry that I hurt you. That thing looks mean. Must have been the seat belt when you hit the curb. Look, you can see the exact outline. Is there anything I can get you? Painkiller? Drink?"

Portia raised her nightgown and covered herself, as though not seeing the dark contusion would lessen the hurt. She turned toward Grover.

"How about some wine?" she replied. "I think there is some cold Pinot Grigio in the fridge."

Grover pulled on his shorts and hurried to the kitchen, returning quickly with wine bottle and glasses. They moved to the settee near the window, where Portia curled up in the corner and Grover poured two generous portions. They drank in silence for a few moments, hearing the subdued whirr, whistle, and cackle of nighttime creatures going about their business in the grassy slope below the window. Grover turned to look outside and saw a faint glow on the horizon. Must be about five, he thought.

Portia stirred and stretched out her hand to his.

"It's not just that I have a sore chest. Yesterday was a downer in so many ways, but the worst was the House voting the park privatization bill out of committee. I know your boss and many of the progressives will vote against it, but there are so many of the new Bull Moose members sponsoring less government and selling off national assets for a quick buck that I am afraid..."

Grover took his cue and held her lightly, kissing the hollow of her neck.

Grover Merson was the thirty-two-year-old chief of staff for Pert Pewtree, congressional representative from the fourteenth district in New Anglia, encompassing Middletown and environs, where Grover and Portia met. He was also one of the four heirs to the Merson toilet paper fortune, still collecting a tiny royalty each time the little metal arm popped out from the side of the rolling machine to wet-seal a roll of paper. Considering the hygienic needs in those countries still using toilet paper, the millions upon millions of rolls employing the Merson process produced a tidy quarterly stipend for Grover Merson and his siblings. That is why Portia and Grover lived in a lovely townhouse in the outskirts of Georgetown, with enough of a yard to host the nighttime creatures providing the background music to their conversation.

Grover considered his wife's concern. It was well founded.

"Pert has a good nose count, and I confess she's worried. You're right about the "BMs" [Bull Moosers]. They are pushing the leader hard for an up-and-down vote because they think they can pass the bill. The leader is torn because she wants to have a majority of the majority [the "Gingrich Rule"] while the BMs are pushing for an open vote. Either way, it looks like a toss-up, perhaps leaning toward passage of the bill."

Portia sighed and frowned.

"You're not cheering me up at all. I believe I will have a little more wine."

Grover emptied the bottle's remaining wine into her glass. He added, "Remember back in 2014 when Obama proposed in his budget to allocate funds for a study about privatizing the Tennessee Valley Authority—the TVA that Eisenhower referred to as 'creeping socialism'?"

"Sort of."

"That's not surprising, since the plan died a sudden and ignominious death. For all the congressional talk about shrinking government and unburdening ourselves of pork and unneeded assets, the representatives in the states receiving cheap electricity from the TVA reconsidered. Their deeply felt convictions quickly dissolved when it became clear that a profit-making enterprise, beholden to Wall Street and shareholders, would charge more for electricity. The TVA remains unchanged."

"And that consoles me how?" asked Portia.

"Pert and her team of representatives plan to delay a vote on the parks bill through procedural measures so that we can mobilize individual constituents who hate the idea of privatization. I begin on that project tomorrow. Of course, the BMs will be hunting for supporters as well—whoever they might be."

Portia frowned. It was clear, even in the dim light of the bedroom, that she felt Grover's effort might be too little, too late—and she said so.

"Grover, you know that other members of our firm and I have already enlisted all the groups we could think of, from the Sierra Club on down, to tell their representatives what a stupid, shortsighted, lame-brained, idiotic, destructive—did I say stupid?—idea this is. I have knocked on more congressional doors than I can count, finagled more free lunches for staffers than there are seeds on a dandelion, pushed..."

Grover looked at his fuming wife and pressed his forefinger to her lips. She exhaled and gave him a doleful look. Doleful, but not defeated; Portia was made of stern stuff.

"Listen, I know all that—and I know your work has been very effective. The scuttlebutt is that a lot of heavyweight lobbyists are pissed at the way you are thwarting their efforts. All I'm saying is that I will be reaching out to networks of individual constituents to make their voices heard. Kind of a GOTV program. It's not too late."

Portia, focusing on her painful chest and slightly muzzy from the late hour and wine, forgot what the "GOTV" acronym meant. She looked quizzically at Grover.

"'Get out the vote.' We have a super database derived from legal new cloud-penetrating software, licensed from NASA, which lets us keep ahead of Apple, Google, Twitter, Natter, and Fundust to harvest the information voters keep in the cloud. And Facebook II offers all that data on a silver platter. I have the z-mails and addresses of millions of individuals who are likely to be disgusted with the idea of privatized parks. Best of all, I am authorized to hire Doctor Phree, the graphic artist who created the hologram of *Werewolf Apocalypse* that blew viewers away during Super Bowl XLVIX. He is on our side and promises an equally compelling message to direct to fobs throughout the country. I'm convinced we can portray its sponsors in such negative light that it will stop the bill in its tracks."

By now, dawn's rosy light crept into their bedroom, glinting off their fobs on the dresser. Grover's enthusiastic sales pitch mollified Portia, who was now trying to decide whether it was worthwhile to crawl back into bed to try for a bit more sleep, hoping to shake the fatigue that still gripped her. Grover, fully awake, moved to the bathing room, pressed the coffee dispenser button, and pulled his razor from its cubbyhole. Portia adjusted the mattress control to her favorite position and returned to the softly humming bed. After a few moments of failing to find a comfortable position, she decided it was no use and rose, eyes still red rimmed, to join Grover and begin washing herself.

After passing the cleansing wand around her mouth she recalled her conversation with her grandfather, remembering the words he used that disturbed her.

"Did I tell you I talked with Wylie yesterday?"

"Don't think so. Anything I should know?"

"Nothing special, although he said something that worried me."

"How so?"

She turned so Grover could fasten the graphite clasp of her bra.

"Well, he referred to Senator Rowe as 'shit dad,' what he used to call him when they were fighting in Korea together."

"And that bothered you?"

"Yes. He often slips back to early times these days—before he corrects himself. It brings me up sharp, and I wonder if he's slowing down. Mentally, you know."

"Come on—how old is Wylie now? Eighty-six, eighty-seven? He's certainly entitled to occasional forgetfulness. Shit, you and I forget stuff all the time."

Portia cast her head to one side, thoughtful.

"I'm sure you're right."

Pause.

"Give me a sip of that coffee."

BATTLE LINES

Sneath's rosy, rotund body, completely submerged in the faux granite whirl-pool of the Capitol Arms Hotel's Vice Presidential Suite bathing room, convulsed slightly as the escape of excess gas resolved a fleeting stomach pain. Susan Spraddle, his executive assistant and occasional bedmate, noted the stream of bubbles popping through the surface, gracing the room with aromatic puffs.

"Jeez, baby, you gotta lay off the pepperoni and garlic at those fancy lunches of yours," she said as she applied a dab of perfume to the crevice between her large, well-proportioned breasts.

Being submerged, Sneath heard none of this, but he opened his eyes to see the watery image of lovely Susan standing next to the tub, clothed only in the antique eyeglasses she favored. His eyes lingered only briefly on her deep blue eyes and cupid bow lips, then wandered slowly over all her lavish assets on display. He emerged from the bath, water dripping from all appendages, intent on refreshing his intimate knowledge of her, but she backed away. That is, she turned her back to him and sped from the room, offering a glimpse of her Botticelli bottom, a view that intensified Sneath's ardor.

Alas, by the time he was toweled and mostly dry, Susan stood, fully clothed with attaché case in hand, at the door, prepared to leave.

"Don't forget—you have a meeting at eleven with Ron Snecker about the parks thing, and you promised your wife to pick up the kids at four. Don't forget."

The door closed quickly, and Sneath stood, slightly moist, in the foyer of the room, searching for his undershorts and cheerfully pondering the day's forthcoming events.

A former three-term representative from North Dakota, Congressman Naydir succumbed to the prospect of riches well beyond the $237,000 (plus perks) he collected as his state's sole representative in the House. North Dakota's population permitted but one representative, although it supported two senators—an irony not lost on Sneath or his detractors in the House. In his fifth year as an elected representative, he concluded that he would rather be dispensing than begging for the largess provided to members of the governing class. He found it burdensome to make almost daily visits to his political office above a Laundromat on M Street to dial for dollars—a quaint expression since he actually spoke the name of the intended donor to his fob. And monthly trips to Bismarck or Fargo wore him out.

Responding to certain overtures, Phylander Musti soon offered Sneath a position with his blue stocking lobbying firm, arranging for interim employment with Americans for Americans, an ultra-conservative not-for-profit political action group funded by the Crouch triplets. By working there for 366 days after resigning his office, he satisfied the annoying "revolving door" strictures of post-congressional employment and became a newly minted member of Musti's lobbying organization.

The very same Crouch triplets then asked Sneath to take on the "parks legislation." The farsighted triplets had, in the front of their minds, the acquisition of Glacier and Yellowstone parks in Montana while reserving the possibility of acquiring even more national parks. To begin, they intended to exploit the tremendous volcanic energy underlying Yellowstone and the numerous rare minerals they had secretly discovered at Glacier. They did not advise Sneath or Musti of their goals. The lobbyists' generous paychecks dissolved concerns about pernicious motives. Sneath forged ahead, doing his best to provide support and succor to the champions of park privatization.

Today's meeting with Ron Snecker would, he hoped, pave the way for inclusion of desired language in the proposed act that was working its way through the Senate. Ron, as senior adviser to Senator Hazard, was influential among the legislators of the "4-H Club," the informal bloc of Senators Hatchett, Hazard, Horowitz, and Hinckle, who received a combined score of 430 percent from the American Conservative Union. So firmly encrusted were their views that attacks by crowbars of reason and fact were easily repulsed. Their service to the Senate was legendary. In hindsight, their positions and demands for action were uniformly wrong. They were negative bellwethers who nevertheless were reelected at the end of their six-year terms. Even Sneath could not understand why that happened.

Ron, bespectacled, sallow, and sporting a crew cut, greeted Sneath in the anteroom to the senator's chambers, oozing false bonhomie.

"Hey, buddy, howzit goin'? Getting' much these days?"

"You betcha!" said Sneath.

The preliminaries out of the way, the two men moved to a small office where Sneath directed his fob to transfer a document to the transceiver on the desk. Two slim pages displayed on the desktop monitor. Ron examined them with furrowed brow.

"You guys don't want much, do you?" he exclaimed sarcastically.

Sneath was prepared.

"Look, we all know that our constituents' interests will be ill served if the post-sale ten-year prohibition against commercial development of the parks is unaltered. If you click the link that points to the Pew survey, you will see that the maximum populace memory scale dwindles to almost nothing after 4.1 years. How many people can recall who lost the vice presidency in the last election? Same thing with the strictures of legislation. Five years from now no one but a few left-wing pundits will remember the original wording of the act, and the Channel Fifteen Paul Ryan news network will eviscerate them."

Ron looked dubious.

"Are you suggesting that we just plan to ignore the prohibition?"

Sneath looked like a wounded doe. His integrity had been attacked.

"Certainly not. Just check the highlighted language of the amendment. There—buried under Section IV, A, ix, c (7)—where it says 'the aforesaid prohibition shall become effective with full force and effect upon ratification by a majority of both houses of Congress within a period of eighteen months after the devolution of the act.'"

"Devolution?" Ron said dubiously.

"Well, perhaps we need a better word."

As Sneath knew, Ron fell into the category of those who swallow the elephant and strain at the gnat. He accepted the idea of an amendment that would vitiate an important section of the proposed act, while deeply pondering a single word. Mulling continued apace. They settled on "initiation."

Ron assured Sneath he would insert the proposed language in the final draft of the bill propounded by the 4-H Club. The conversation then turned to the honorarium his boss would receive for addressing the Mothers for Americans symposium on the immorality of the highly effective "fortnight after" birth control pill. It would be generous since "Mothers" was an offshoot of Americans for Americans and enjoyed the almost limitless generosity of the Crouch triplets.

Ron expressed his contentment with the arrangements concluded and Sneath departed. Alone in the elevator to the lobby of the Senate chambers, he punched the air above, executed a little two-step, and mouthed a drawn out "yessss!"

Agatha Jackson stared angrily at the words streaming across the monitor bar of her desk. The greeny yellow characters spelled out, in teen-pop shorthand, the potential demise of her department and her career.

Moments before, Noble Ferrari, secretary of the Interior, had advised her that he had every confidence in her ability to deleverage the department's real property holdings, should congressional action so require.

She sat with elbows on the desk, her head in her hands, curly black hair spilling over her dark eyes. As director of the National Park Service, a title earned through over twenty-five years of passionate and dedicated service to the department, her superior just told her it would be her responsibility to arrange for the sale of her beloved parks.

That was, if those assholes on Capitol Hill in their supreme idiocy decided to auction off the pride of the nation's patrimony, almost four percent of the country's land mass. She had read the arguments for the sale. Dysfunctional government had been unable to address the crumbling national infrastructure, the diminishing intellectual accomplishments of its students, health issues caused by the repeal of the Affordable Care Act, and the rapidly rising poverty level in the country. Many economists proclaimed that, in spite of the government's creative accounting, the nation was teetering on the brink of bankruptcy.

Accordingly, Congress seized upon the multitrillion-dollar asset of the national parks to provide a quick fix to the issues that threatened the nation and, incidentally, also threatened to unseat its members. The brush of discontent tarred both parties. The unthinkable, as far as Agatha Jackson was concerned, might become a reality.

The greeny yellow letters crossing her screen announced that the "parks bill" had cleared the House committee and would be taken up as soon as the members completed one of their quadrennial two-week vacations. Agatha, seeking help in any port from this congressional storm, reached for her fob.

"Please call Portia Merson."

Moments before receiving the call from Agatha, Portia had made a confusing discovery. Worried about unaccustomed fatigue and peculiar mood swings, she had squeezed a drop of her blood into the app on her fob and discovered she was pregnant.

Her initial surprise quickly gave way to elation. Although she and Grover had used birth control during the early months of their marriage, lately, as though by unspoken consent, they were not so careful. So, she was not surprised that their devil-may-care attitude resulted in this—a maroon plus sign supported by romantic violin sounds blinking on the screen in her hand. A massive grin appeared as Portia became thoroughly pleased with herself. Motherhood, she thought—what a concept!

She immediately decided to share her joy with Grover and instinctively clicked his icon on the fob, only to cancel the call a moment later. No, she thought, this disembodied communication would not do to announce the pending arrival of their first child. Better to wait until they were together at their home to make the announcement. She was thinking about appropriate words when her fob announced Agatha's call. The right words for Grover could wait. She knew what her friend must be calling about.

Agatha blew past introductory comments and came immediately to the point."Ferrari just made it clear that I will be the point person in auctioning off the parks if it comes to that. He made it sound like a great opportunity, that S.O.B. Here I am—spent almost a lifetime fighting discrimination all the way developing the parks programs—and I'm supposed to preside not only over their demise but that of my job as well. Just thinking about all the people who will lose their jobs makes me scream. And Ferrari will remain above it all. That presidential appointee is so crooked he can chew nails and spit corkscrews! C'mon girlfriend, let me know how it's going with you. Give me some hope."

Portia had complete sympathy for her friend. Although Agatha was many years older, they formed a strong bond over the parks issue, both working to avoid the destruction of a national institution that preserved much of the country's natural beauty and elevated the spirit of so many Americans. Portia brought Agatha up to date about the strategies the various parks' champions were pursuing.

"While the legislature is on vacation again, Agatha, it's going to be a full-court press by our people. Senator Rowe and Representative Pewtree are leading the charge. I am also working to challenge the 4-H Club. I believe that at least one of them is vulnerable."

More, Portia could not then say. Agatha, mollified, said good-bye, and Portia alternated her thoughts between the new life in her body and the various ways she planned to save the parks.

Wylie took the transporter from the George W. Bush heliport near the new Senate Office Building to the office of his old friend, Senator Pierre (now "Pete") Rowe, the senior senator from Louisiana—known as the "Cagey Cajun." They had been friends since perilous days during the Korean War. Now in their late eighties, active but careful in choosing their pursuits, they had shared all their secrets, joys, and disappointments. They treated each of their meetings as a precious gift to be savored. Future meetings were never assured.

Rowe rose slowly from his desk to meet Wylie at the entrance to his office. Their tentative movements belied earlier days when they had dodged Chinese mortar shells and scrambled across forbidden territory in a damaged jeep expertly piloted by Private Rowe. The vintage Private Rowe clasped Wylie's hand in both of his and motioned his friend to one of two leather chairs next to a coffee table in the corner of his expansive office. Wylie noticed that the senator was using his cane again. Rowe noticed that his friend seemed a bit more stooped than before. The two old men settled comfortably in the chairs, each producing a little sigh of contentment.

They proceeded with their habitual litany of reports about family members, beginning with their wives, both of whom were well. As they worked their way down to grandchildren, Wylie remarked that Portia had questioned him again about the Parks Act.

"Damn stupid business," said Rowe, adding, "Portia's a good operator, a quick study, and has learned her way around the hill. I keep my eye on her, you know. Good girl, and that Grover—he's a comer. Bright future, both of them. Peckerheads in the House and in our chamber, like those 4-Hers, that's a real problem. Gonna be close, but I'm helpin' where I can."

Wylie was pleased to know that his friend was "on the case," and appreciated his favorable appraisal of his granddaughter. He leaned closer.

"I've made a few calls to the environmental groups I represent. We can count on additional help from that quarter, and a bit of funding too. We can't let the big business lobby win this one. I am still smarting over the shoddy construction of the Keystone XL pipeline and the fires and oil pollution from that fiasco!"

The senator nodded.

"Made an unholy mess of our beloved coastline. Damn near wiped out our brown pelicans."

They calmed down and, on cue, Rowe's principle assistant, Zelda Barnickle, arrived with scotch for Wylie and tea for her boss. The senator's cardiologist had ruled out hard liquor years earlier. Wylie, however, could enjoy one and a half ounces of Glenmorangie daily. They sipped and talked of bygone days. For reasons he could not understand, Wylie discovered that his eyes were wet with tears.

VIRTUAL REALITY

Melvin Salmon, scrawny and intense computer savant, did not think of himself as a stalker. He fashioned himself as misunderstood denizen of an earlier age, when sex, pot, and rock and roll ruled. He was in his late 20's, slender in build and passably handsome, with reddish hair and a slight chin curtain. He simply had an inordinate interest in Portia Merson, whom he respected and honored for representing him a few years earlier. She defended him pro bono after his arrest for hacking his college network and publicizing the answers to a reproductive biology exam. Portia argued that the college had a duty to encrypt the data so that an idiot savant like Melvin could not so easily crack the code. The judge agreed and released him, and Melvin promised, henceforth, to leave the college data alone.

Instead, he pursued two passions: creating the first erotic Internet game in which players selected their own avatars to have sex with other avatars, and educating himself on every available aspect of Portia's life and career. He limited actual contact to sending Portia a card every Christmas, signed "fondly, a secret admirer."

His internet game, AEROTICA, was an instant success. In no time, he joined the ranks of other Internet millionaires and hired programmers to enhance the game's appeal by creating even more exotic avatars, including children with large, soulful eyes.

Contrary to the game's published promise to keep players' confidential information sacrosanct—private as a tomb—Melvin sometimes, for his own amusement, followed the activities of renowned or celebrity players. Thus, he developed comprehensive files on luminaries including a Supreme Court justice, five dozen members of Congress (of both sexes), male movie stars of various ages, moguls of industry, titans of legal, medical, and accounting practices, etc. Of the millions of players routinely depositing bitcoins to enjoy their fetishes, a few caught his fancy. Occasionally his fascination with Portia's well-being resulted in the discovery of tidbits of information about certain players that could work to Portia's benefit. One such person was Senator Porter Hinckle.

Hinckle, a Bible-thumping family values firebrand, believed that big government was what ailed the country, making that point in all his speeches, lambasting all federal officers, demanding the abolition of those agencies whose names he could remember. Meanwhile, as an elected member of government, he collected his biweekly paycheck and enjoyed the benefits of a federally funded staff and other generous perquisites. Irony was lost on Hinckle.

Baser instincts, however, were not. He was too careful of his position to risk the activities he enjoyed earlier in life as he clawed his way up the political ladder. The guilty and secret pleasure of playing AEROTICA, however, provided needed release. His favorite guise was that of a satyr who deflowered young boys and girls. When he donned his third-edition Oculus Rift headset, the sensation of chase, struggle, and conquest was so palpable it was as though he felt tender flesh in his hands. The denouement always provided a happy ending.

What first brought Porter Hinckle to Melvin Salmon's attention was a visit from Amanda Floss, an FBI agent working in the New York Exceptional Victims Department.

Amanda had won her spurs heading the pederasty unit, whose members posed as runaway teens yearning for acceptance and understanding in Internet postings. Perpetrators who rose to that bait were encouraged to exchange smutty xxxmails, and assignations were arranged. Those caught in the Internet net were charged with endangerment of a minor and, if the FBI had provided explicit photos, child pornography.

That program had run its course, however, when perpetrators with money hired a high-powered attorney who argued entrapment in Federal District Court. The government, reluctantly representing the FBI, lost in district and appellate courts, and a number of perpetrators whose lives had been ruined were suing for damages of extraordinary amounts.

Nevertheless, the Department promoted Amanda Floss to head a new unit charged with ferreting out cyber deviants.

The reason she gave when making an appointment with Melvin was to seek his cooperation in identifying the 1,213 players of AEROTICA her department had branded as potential sexual deviants—based on the violent games they played.

Amanda bustled into his cluttered office and displayed her identity confirmer. Large and stocky, twice Melvin's size, wearing an unfashionable red dress, she resembled the little engine that could trying to crest a hill. Refusing to sit, she moved close to Melvin's desk and drew herself up to full height, trying to dominate him. She pulled out her shiny, last generation Government Issue fob and projected a list of names, highlighted in shocking pink, on his desktop. Melvin looked over the list.

"So, let me get this straight…the FBI wants me to give you the real names of the people whose aliases appear on this list?"

"Absolutely correct!"

"I thought you people were like cops—uphold the law, serve and protect, all that."

"You got that right."

"So you must know about the Internet Privacy Act."

"Sure. It doesn't apply to sexual deviants, though."

Melvin thought a moment.

"Uh, you don't know whether these people **are** sexual deviants, so even if the Internet Privacy Act doesn't apply, neither of us now knows to whom it doesn't apply. That's a conundrum. So, even if you're right, I couldn't divulge that information since I could be violating the act regarding people who are not sexual deviants. Right?

Amanda seemed confused by Melvin's logic.

"Don't bust my balls!" she said. "The damn act doesn't apply to sexual deviants, and that's that."

Melvin pointed his fob at the desk, unscrolling a copy of the Privacy Act.

"OK, if you say so. Do me a favor, just for my edification, show me where it says that in the act."

Amanda settled her hefty bulk on the corner of the desk, glanced balefully at Melvin, pulled the latest Google monocle from her pocket, carefully screwed in into her left eye socket, and began to run her finger down the text of the act.

Melvin fought to restrain his glee. No way in hell was there an exemption in the act for "deviants." Amanda maintained her act for a few moments more, and then turned toward Melvin.

"Can't find it right now. You know how tricky legal language is. Need to be a lawyer to figure that out."

(Amanda was a lawyer.)

She leaned toward Melvin, fixing him with her best dominating glare.

"So, you telling me you're not going to cooperate?"

"Not till pigs fly over Hell's frozen landscape."

She pulled herself up and strode to the door.

"I'll be back," she intoned, Schwarzenegger style.

Melvin laughed aloud as Amanda slammed the door.

He looked again at Amanda's list. Hinckle's alias, "Honeybuckets," was seventh from the top. That was how Melvin began to develop a special interest in Senator Porter Hinckle. It was not long before the inventive and curious Melvin realized he had information about the fourth member of the 4-H Club that would aid Portia in her battle to scuttle the parks legislation. He just had to figure out the best way to implement a program of blackmail.

Grover beamed a million-dollar lottery winner smile. While beaming, he rushed to Portia and enveloped her in a massive happy bear hug, reconsidered, held her at arm's length, and involuntarily looked toward her lean belly. It was Portia's turn to smile.

"There won't be anything to see there for a couple of months, at least. But you'll probably enjoy that my boobs will enlarge and that I'll become ravenous for sex."

Grover seemed surprised.

"Ravenous?"

"I kinda made that part up, but the boobs will grow. That's been confirmed by a couple of my friends—and from the eleventh edition of *What to Expect When You're Expecting*. I'm just hoping I can escape the morning sickness part."

"Oh. Morning sickness."

"Yes. Projectile barfing."

"Doesn't sound so good when you put it that way."

"Not looking forward to it."

By now, they were sitting together on the couch, and Grover was exploring the promise of breast growth, causing Portia to giggle slightly as he frowned at the lack of instant development.

Earlier, Portia had returned home from work before Grover, inserted two all-natural gourmet chicken Kiev meals in the Instachef, clicked it on, and read the package label to be sure all would be ready when Grover said he would be home. She found real candles in the cupboard reserved for unused wedding gifts and prepared the dining table for the meal. Red wine for Grover, raspberry grape juice for her. No alcohol to mess up her first born—forget what Harvard Med said about their discovery that wheat beer helped the fetus thrive.

Though preoccupied with the day's work developments, Grover knew something was out of the ordinary when he saw the candles. Portia quickly joined him, forgot her rehearsed monologue about the coming baby, kissed her husband, and blurted out, "Dammit, Grover, we're pregnant!"

A pole ax to the head would have been less stunning than Portia's news. Grover felt the string go out of his legs, and managed to find a seat on the couch. He swallowed the "how" that almost blurted from his mouth, realizing that he was completely and passionately familiar with the how of it. Disbelief turned to elation, and he rose to hug the wonderful woman who would be the mother of his first child.

It was some time before their conversation turned to the events of their working lives. Even then, Grover interjected exclamations of delight at the prospect of fatherhood, envisioning teaching his son to play with various kinds of balls, taking him on long walks, swimming, bike riding…

"Calm down, big boy," said Portia. "There's a better than even chance our child will be a girl, according to the statistics I pulled from our ultranet this afternoon. Let's concentrate on having a healthy baby right now."

"Sure. Of course. Right."

Grover paused.

"So how long is it until we can test to tell the baby's sex?"

Portia threw a pillow at his head.

"Senator," said Hinckle's assistant, "there's a scruffy-looking man in the antechamber, no appointment, not even sure how he got past security. Says he would like a 'moment of your time.' Says he would like to talk to you about 'Honeybuckets.' What do you want me to do?"

"Honeybuckets" riveted Porter Hinckle's attention. He turned from his computer desk thoughtfully and said, "Hmmmm. What does he look like?"

"Like I said—scruffy. Has a kind of beard on his chin, real long reddish hair, T-shirt and shorts. Some kind of boots, and he has a canvas satchel full of I don't know what."

"And he said it was about 'Honeybuckets'?"

"That's right. He said to give you his card."

She handed the senator Melvin's holographic card, which showed a slowly rotating "Melvin" under a bold "AEROTICA" in undulating script. Hinckle pressed "Melvin" and Melvin's full name, xmail information, and the slogan "When you need to get beside yourself" appeared.

Glumly, his assistant ushered Melvin into Hinckle's ornate office and reluctantly offered him a chair in front of the senator's mahogany desk— real wood, none of that artificial stuff. As she closed the office door, the senator appeared from the bathing room, rubbing his hands. Melvin was exactly as his assistant had described, except for the rusty sideburns currently fashionable in the artistic community. Melvin remained seated as the senator moved briskly to his leather recliner and said, "What can I do for you?"

Melvin smiled winningly at Hinckle.

"Senator, I have an ethical and legal problem that involves the FBI, you, and me."

Hinckle looked more closely at Melvin. In his experience, no good could come of the combination of words Melvin used.

"Go on."

Taking his time, Melvin explained who he was and recounted Amanda Floss' visit, pointing out that the "Honeybuckets" alias was very close to the top of the list of potential cyber deviants. He asked if the senator would like his memory refreshed, since he had a copy of one of his recent avatar encounters on his fob. The senator declined. Melvin got almost to the point.

"I intended to exercise my constitutional rights under the first and fifth amendments and refuse to disclose the identities of any of my customers. However, that could expose me to time-consuming, costly, and painful litigation. So, I ask myself—is it worth it? Should I really care if my players are engaging in carnal knowledge of unsubstantial teeny-boppers? That's my dilemma. So I am getting in touch with players that I hold in very high regard for their input. Would you give me your guidance?"

Longtime political operator that he was, Hinckle recognized a shakedown as it was about to bite him in the ass. The negotiation had begun; his goal was to reduce his financial and/or political pain as much as possible.

"Well," said Hinckle, "I would stand by any American who exercised his God-given constitutional rights, no matter what. I have built my reputation as a champion of constitutional rights. Yes, I have."

"I am so glad to hear that," noted Melvin. "I guess what I need to know is how forcefully you are prepared to stand by me. It seems to me that I would be risking a lot to protect all my players from the FBI. I don't know...perhaps there is some way you could help me out."

This verbal choreography continued for a while. Hinckle waved aside his assistant's intrusion to remind him of another appointment, and asked, "Well, what specifically do you have in mind?"

Melvin came fully to the point.

"Your support for the parks bill is very unsettling. It seems to me that you are trading political expediency for the glory of our country—a trade than can never be undone. If you could find it in your heart to modify your stance and withdraw your support, I would certainly assert my constitutional rights on *your* behalf. Or, if you prefer, mistakenly identify 'Honeybuckets' to the FBI as one of your political enemies."

Hinckle considered, steepled hands supporting his chin. Was it nobler in the mind, he thought, to suffer the outrageous slanders of the press, the revulsion of his constituents, the mistrust of his family, the slings and arrows of late-night comics—or a sudden lack of support by the three other members of the 4-H Club? He would make his choice. It was Profiles in Courage time.

"All right. I'll come out against the Parks Act. Though it probably won't affect the outcome. The act has solid support."

Melvin shook his head in appreciation.

"That's OK. Every little bit helps. Do me a little favor? Call Portia Merson's office over at the National Green Defense League and let her know about your change of heart? You know, like in the next day or so."

Melvin, in his desire to support his hero, did not realize how great a blunder he had made. Portia's name was now associated with his gambit. Portia and the NGDL would immediately be in the crosshairs of the diverse organizations supporting the Parks Act.

Hinckle could not restrain a smile at receiving this gold chip in the game of politics. So, the scruffy sleazeball sitting across the desk from him favored this Portia person. Interesting. He placed both palms on his desk.

"All right. I'll have one of my people make the call. Now…you'll excuse me."

Melvin nodded ascent and withdrew. In the same elevator that Sneath used for his little victory dance, Melvin took inventory of other influentials on the list of cyber deviates. He was sure he could do more for Portia.

The elation Portia felt when the call came from Senator Hinckle's office was short lived. Unfortunately, the news that one of the 4-H Club stalwarts had surprisingly changed his position on the Parks Act as a matter of conscience came moments before the onset of a shattering bout of nausea. She rushed to the office bathroom and revisited breakfast. Thoughts of congressional conquest temporarily evaporated. The hope of an uneventful first trimester of her pregnancy dimmed.

OPPORTUNITIES ABOUND

The Crouch triplets were conceived in a test tube and nourished in a Petri dish before being relocated to their mother's womb. There they swam in warm amniotic fluid for almost nine months, lulled by the dulcet sounds of *Baby Bartok, Beethoven, and Berlioz* recorded by the Albuquerque chamber orchestra and delivered by the most modern abdominal surround sound speakers.

Their father, Orlando Crouch, scion of a small but prosperous oil, gas, and minerals operation north of Albuquerque, suffered from low sperm count, attributed by his mother to excessive masturbation as a youth. She mistakenly believed that, like eggs for her sex, every man had a finite number of "sperms" available over time and that Orlando simply depleted his supply. Orlando was unsure of her diagnosis, but suffered mother-induced guilt and remorse for some time before his young bride, nee Rebecca Planchet, harvested enough of his essence to allow medical concentration and a happy union with three of her robust eggs.

The expectation was that one or two of the fertilized eggs would normally expire, but Fred, Frank, and Fergus defied the odds and thrived. Orlando greeted their ultimate arrival on a frosty New Mexico night with delight, exulting in proof of his potency, thrilling to the prospect of new blood to grow his business. Rebecca, exhausted, clutched the little bundles of red flesh and speckled hair to her breast, looking into their scrunched-up little faces, suffused with mother love. You will never want for anything, my darlings, she thought. I will see to that.

With such a beginning, it is understandable that the Crouch triplets saw the world as their oyster.

Since a separate egg produced each child, the Crouch triplets were not identical. Fergus resembled Rebecca, and Fred and Frank took after Orlando. They had their childhood disagreements. Fergus had a little scar in his forehead where Frank hit him with a mallet, and Fred suffered two broken wrists when Frank tossed him out of a mesquite tree. Frank became the dominant triplet, leading through fear and intimidation.

When they grew up, Frank concentrated on the oil and gas business. He expanded properties located in the Texas panhandle and moved into Oklahoma and Canada. He set up headquarters in Calgary, Denver, and Houston. After Orlando retired, Frank never had a year without a large profit. He understood balance sheets; if revenue was static or dropped, he managed to cut operating costs, mainly by cheating his employees and lessors and ignoring annoying regulations. Frank knew it was cheaper to adjust regulations in his favor by the generous distribution of political contributions than by compliance.

Fred was detail oriented, finding solace in the predictability of numbers; he became a tax lawyer and received a PMBA from the University of Denver. Fred became an expert in analyzing the business deals that Frank promoted. In his own right, Fred invested in copper, silver, uranium, and coal mines located in the Northwest and in depressed areas of Appalachia. His coal operations generously deposited the remains of mountaintops into valleys below, damming streams and polluting the ones remaining with noxious tailings. His open pit copper mine in Butte, Montana, swallowed part of the town. Through the proper application of political contributions, Frank arranged for the town to move.

Fergus played guitar and gravitated to the arts. He originated the Crouch Charitable Foundation that donated funding for numerous venues for the arts.

He commissioned I.M. Pei's daughter to design the Crouch Pavilion, which featured so prominently at the annual Albuquerque balloon festivals.

The timber business appealed to Fergus. He acquired timber properties in Maine, Tennessee, Kentucky, and Georgia, and thousands of acres of leases from the Bureau of Land Management. On leased properties, his annual stumpage count was always significantly less than expected by the federal land managers. Because Congress continually underfunded the Bureau, the overworked BLM managers' concerns were noted and ignored. BLM workers decided that the Crouch Timber Division was either the least-efficient operator on the planet or run by cheating, lying bastards. Fergus cared not; profits rolled on in.

When the triplets were in their mid-forties their origins as separate little zygotes became apparent. Frank resembled a balding embodiment of any child's fearful image of Ebenezer Scrooge. Fred, taller, with hair and pleasant looking, seemed more like a shoe salesman than a titan of industry. He was slow to anger and low key. Fergus, the shortest brother, resembled a stretched out pat of butter with sorrowful brown eyes. He melted easily under Frank's scorn. However, their combined business acumen and dedicated application to profits at any cost created a mutual net worth of over seventeen billion new dollars. They, their wives (first for Fred and Fergus, third for Frank), and children thrived under a golden shower of excess, enjoying the benefits of the truly rich.

One of those benefits was the exercise, in corporate guise, of their First Amendment rights of absolute freedom of speech. Decisions of the "Mitch" McConnell Supreme Court following *Citizens United* and *Hobby Lobby*, particularly *Condoms 'R' Us* and *Unplanned Parenthood*, guaranteed that the Crouch Corporation could spend as much money as it wished to influence legislators and elections, without disclosing any of those contributions.

At a meeting at their Houston headquarters, Fred reviewed the latest ruling that dealt with corporate political contributions, *Ferguson v. Plessy Amalgamated*.

"Under this decision," said Fred, "large corporations are determined to be more equal than ordinary citizens by virtue of their size, the large number of people in their employ, the status of their executives in the world community, and their ability to contribute to the economy of the nation through their payment of substantial taxes. Consequently, to discourage such entities from moving more of their funds offshore, thereby avoiding or delaying tax payments, the court upheld the administration's policy decision to consider corporate political contributions as legitimate and deductible business expenses."

Fergus chuckled. "Great! Now we get to deduct the money we spent to get the administration to approve the tax change."

Frank, momentarily distracted, said, "Tell me again how that deduction works. Since we don't have to disclose the amounts we spend on political contributions, does the IRS check the actual contribution amounts?"

"It's 'trust but let someone else verify,'" Fred acknowledged. "We just pay one of the remaining Big Three accounting firms to check the books and, ka-ching, we are home free."

"Oh, like in the last precious metal bubble. We pay the fox to count the chickens."

"Yes, something like that," agreed Fred.

Fred paused, letting his brothers ruminate about the new political reality. He added, "Today, free speech equals money. In other words, we now have the Supreme Court's confirmation of the old business adage—'Money Talks.' God bless the Supreme Court."

Although this was not fresh news to Frank, he raised himself in his chair and said, "Yessir! That's the way it needs to be. We're the less than one percent and our founding fathers understood that we should have special rights to influence how things work in America. What you're saying, Fred, is that we can now spend unlimited money to target anyone we want with our messages of what is right? That we can support any wingnut we favor for Congress, not have to record it, and write it off as a business expense? That's fabulous."

"How about gifts to legislators and government employees?" asked Fergus. "Can we do better there?"

"I'm afraid not," said Fred. "We got tagged pretty bad with all those free corporate jet rides and no-attendance-necessary three-day couples conferences in Las Vegas, Paris, and London last year. I'm trying to figure out how to help the Congress people who have to pay us back for that stuff. It's tough. The IRS, underfunded as it is, is keeping a sharp eye on us. But I am always open to creative thinking and new ideas. Our legal team is working on it, of course."

Frank indulged in a selfish grin and walked to the glass expanse of windows in the office. He looked lovingly at the clogged arteries of highway below, the whisper of industrial haze that shrouded the gleaming buildings before them, the artificial turf that showed improbably green on the little parks in the distance. The Crouch Stadium with its massive wing-like carbon fiber and titanium roof stood like a rampart two blocks from their offices.

They had done so much for Houston, for the country. They had kept the progressives, the free thinkers, the perverse scientists, the voodoo economists, the bleeding-heart liberals, at bay. Just think of what their money, their political freedom, their business expertise could do to keep the country on the right path and, coincidentally, support their operations.

Frank turned back toward his brothers,

"OK, enough self-congratulation. Let's figure out how we can stop all this negative talk about our enhanced fracking process. It's affecting operations in Canada and Oklahoma. It's like that old 'whack-a-mole' game we used to play. You put to rest one city's bitching about how we've ruined their water supply, and another pops up somewhere else. Does anyone really give a crap that Wichita is experiencing a four-times-normal stomach cancer rate among its under-five population?"

His brothers shook their heads in agreement. As far as they were concerned, nobody should give a crap or anything else. Frank went on.

"Anyway, how are we doing, Fred, with that medical study we funded to show that the chemicals we use in fracking are harmless?"

Fred scratched his head.

"The medical team says it is hard to complete the study without our disclosing exactly what chemicals we use. That category of 'other' isn't helpful. They are thinking of backing out."

"Damn!" cried Frank. "Fire that guy who used to run the CDC and bring in a more pliable foreign doctor. I want that study completed this year—no matter what it costs."

Fergus offered, "I don't know about that. You can't get a baby in a month by getting nine women pregnant."

Frank bristled.

"And your point is?"

"Just saying."

Frank chose to ignore his brother. He walked back to his chair at the head of the conference table and sorted through notes on a soiled napkin he pulled from his pocket.

"Oh, yeah. What are we doing to stop that blonde in the pink sneakers who's running for Texas governor *again*?"

THE NEW OLD

Senator Rowe leaned toward the chair Wylie occupied and loosened his belt for comfort before snatching two pigs in a blanket from the tray his assistant placed on the edge of his desk. Although hard liquor was taboo, he could still enjoy an afternoon snack. He deftly dredged the appetizer through a puddle of barbecue sauce, resisted the impulse to stuff the entire little sausage in his mouth, took a small bite, and began the harangue Wiley knew would be coming.

"Those Crouch triplets, they're a scourge on the nation. Making a mockery of our political system with fistfuls of unregulated money. There's not a single one of our thirty-two Republican governors who doesn't have a ton of Crouch money stashed in his or her personal coffers. And now they're sticking their noses right into local matters. Even down in my parishes their people are acting like scallywag carpetbaggers. Unrecorded spending of Crouch dollars to elect local officials, even school board members, who lean to the far right of Attila the Hun. Or, they shove money to local committees trying to defeat good people who know a thing or two about what's really going on. Wylie, they're gumming the works; it's essasperatin'!"

Wylie had heard that Crouch operatives were tinkering with his friend's well-oiled Louisiana political operations, so the senator's complaints were no surprise.

"Well, you can't blame them," he said. "What with Congress, in spite of your good efforts, maintaining its course of perennial gridlock, and only taking action to allow rudimentary functioning of government, states and municipalities have tried to pick up the slack. They are doing their best to improve the lot of immigrants, provide better education for the poor, grant a living wage, and offer a hodgepodge of medical services after the Affordable Care Act was gutted. With more decisions made at lower levels of government, the Crouches need to expand their influence at that level. And it looks like they are doing it."

"You're right," the senator added bitterly. "You notice how quickly the National Infrastructure Act got funded as soon as Crouch Industries expanded into highway and bridge construction?"

"Well, at least that should put a stop to all those cars and trucks falling through bridges," Wylie noted.

The two old men continued venting about the parlous state of the national economy. Their concerns were justified. As the nation's economy stuttered and stumbled, it was impossible for many elements of a functioning society to operate efficiently when Congress's idea of planning was funding the Department of Defense in two-month increments. Worry that the government might not be able to pay its bills or continue to borrow to fund peacekeeping missions in Columbia, Malaysia, and Switzerland took its toll. Economists from left and right predicted the unheard of—bankruptcy. Worse than in Italy, UK, Australia, and Brazil.

With this background, the Parks Act managed to work its way out of committee. Elections were coming and the mood of the voting public was even more negative than usual. With an almost zero percent approval rating, incumbents were restive. There was a real chance that the customary ninety percent reelection of incumbent representatives could drop to seventy, even sixty, percent. The prospect that as many as 170 legislators could lose their salaries and benefits for the ninety-eight days a year they were in session was devastating.

Something must be done.

The Parks Act became a shining beacon, a measure that would permit the squabbling minority to gain many of its long-held objectives, provide proper business management of an underused government asset, plump up the sagging national coffers, and, most important, demonstrate to the public that their legislators were worth their pay. They could do **something**.

A more portly Frank Crouch settled into his conference room chair and nodded noncommittally to his brothers as they absorbed the business data displayed on the grayed-out window wall facing the stadium. The numbers dancing across his line of vision fascinated Fred; he enjoyed them even more than watching his beloved Puffins in combat on his interactive 3D picture wall.

Fergus quickly grew bored. He had examined the consolidated balance sheet and cash flow statements and noted their net worth had gained an additional two billion for the quarter. He thought about designing a new building to house his antique kinescope collection. He was personally involved in cataloging and transferring the *Howdy Doody* tapes, now brittle with age, to new platinum DDT disks. He loved that program, frequently remarking to his wife, "They don't make them like that anymore." He was convinced that Buffalo Bob was an underappreciated talent, and wished he had met the puppeteer who made Howdy so alive.

Frank cleared his throat with a gravelly sound and pointed to an area of interest with his fob.

"That long-range forecast shows continuing drought in the Southwest. Columbia River's almost petered out. Water's going to be the hottest commodity out there; give it a couple more years or so."

His brothers agreed, unsure where Frank was going with this.

"We need to focus on the Parks Act that our people have so carefully steered through the House. My latest information is that it's close, and that we can get it on the president's desk in three, maybe four, months."

"That long?" asked Fred.

"You kidding?" Fergus chimed in. "That's like lightning these days."

As customary, Frank ignored the background chatter.

"Look, I have personally urged our chief lobbyist, Sneath Naydir, to help clear the way for us to gain an interest in Yellowstone and Glacier. You both have the memo on that. However, I think we should consider the Grand Canyon too—instead of Glacier even. Just imagine…"

Fergus yawned behind his hand, obviously more interested in the Crouch commercial with the near-naked girl extolling Crouch Resorts playing on the window wall. Frank leaned over the table and slapped Fergus, hard, atop his head. His brother snapped to attention.

"Just imagine," he continued, "damming the canyon—damming the biggest canyon in the world—collecting and controlling trillions of gallons of clean water in the Colorado River, water from the Rockies, best water in the country. Eventually the water would be priceless!"

"I'm not sure that would be legal, Frank. Not like that's permitted in the act," said Fred.

Still smarting from his slapped head, Fergus added, "Right. Doesn't sound legal."

Frank adopted a look of imperious disbelief.

"Listen, butthead, our environmental counsel has researched this and discovered that there is plenty of precedent for the idea of bookend dams for the Grand Canyon. There have been plans in place since early in the twentieth century. It almost happened back in the 1960s when the Interior Department announced plans to build a pair of dams across the Colorado River. One of the many advantages cited was…"

Here Frank clicked his fob to reviewed information on a page outlined in red.

"Yes…they claimed that by filling the canyon with water, more people than ever could see its walls from boats. But those pissants at the Sierra Club got into it and lobbied hard—so hard that the IRS suspended their tax-exempt status for breaking rules against political lobbying. Anyway, the club generated so much heat that the government scrapped the plan in 1968."

"So, wait," said Fergus. "Do we need to worry about losing the tax exemption for our UltraPACs?"

"No," asserted Fred." That's been settled. Congress decided the underfunded IRS has better things to do than go after billions of dollars they could collect from law-abiding Political Action Committees. Remember, 'money equals speech.'"

"Getting you two to stay on track is harder than herding cats!" Frank said. "What I want to get across here is the feasibility of the Grand Canyon project. We even have the detailed plans to dam the Colorado River."

Frank flashed a copy of one of the original engineering drawings on the wall to demonstrate his point. His brothers reviewed the plans, guessing at the profits their construction divisions would generate. They assumed that Crouch Construction would be the winning bidder.

Fred asked, "Done any analysis of the cash flow of such a project, Frankie?"

Frank detested "Frankie." He cursed at his brother for lapsing into the diminutive. Chastened, Fred kept quiet, insecure in the knowledge that Frank would soon extract revenge for his lapse.

"Of course we ran the numbers. ROI is somewhere between astronomical and infinite. Listen, right now people all over the country are wandering into supermarkets and convenience stores and plunking down hard cash to pay four times more for bottled water than they pay for gasoline. Who's going to be squeamish about paying, say, just a little more for water than gas to have it delivered to their homes and farms and businesses? Nobody, that's who!"

Fred and Fergus offered no counterarguments. The meeting ended. Fergus continued to focus on the slightly clad young women appearing on the commercial loop on the wall, and a worried Fred returned to his corner office, wondering how his brother would punish him. How many times, he asked himself, had Frank reminded him that he didn't get mad; he got even.

STRANGE BEDFELLOWS

Tureen O'Porto enjoyed the looks she received on entering a new office venue, which she did often as one of K Street's most effective and well-paid lobbyists. Tall and shapely, with hair as red as a cardinal shrub in fall and eyes bluer than the Aegean Sea, she projected power and influence. Yet, even in her sharply tailored Lady Armani suit, she also projected a raw sexuality immediately noted by all the men in the office who secretly subscribed to *Hologram Hustler*. That is, almost all the men in the office. Many of them became slack jawed when she entered, usually turning away with a sly smile. Women responded with envy, jealousy, and attraction. All eyes turned to Tureen O'Porto as she entered the offices of the National Green Defense League.

The product of a summer romance between an Irish graduate student cataloging gravestones in Salamanca and the son of a prosperous Portuguese vintner, Tureen spent an enchanted childhood among the gilded vineyards by the Douro River and the bracing Irish highlands. When she was twelve, her parents settled in the United States, where her father imported the finest Port wines from his country and established exclusive fine wine boutiques throughout the country.

Business thrived and Tureen, aided by her beauty and brilliance, was educated at Deerfield Academy and Dartmouth College. Upon graduation from Harvard Business and Law schools, she married Violet Armagasson, her best friend from Dartmouth, but the marriage did not last. Tureen could not be limited to a single partner or sexual identity.

Now, she turned her face, brilliant teeth, and azure eyes set in a tanned matrix of smooth skin toward the male receptionist, already reduced to a puddle of submission.

"I have an appointment with Portia Merson," she said. "Please let her know I am here."

The receptionist ushered Tureen into a small, spare conference room, one of the few rooms in the office with a view of the outside. Compared with the plush offices at her firm, the room was shabby, uninviting. She seated herself on an upholstered metal chair and placed her Dior folio on a battered oak table, the main fixture of the room. She crossed her silken legs, waiting.

Preserve me forever from working in the not-for-profit world, she thought, feeling as though the room was conspiring to cover her with invisible grit.

Portia, looking tired and wan, soon entered. She had just returned from the bathing room for her second expulsive experience of the morning, and damp ringlets of brown hair clung to her forehead. She apologized for being a bit tardy.

"I pride myself on being able to organize most things, but morning sickness is not one of them," she said ruefully, instantly gaining Tureen's attention and creating feminine solidarity. "What can I do for you?"

The question was more than a formality. Portia wondered for two days what this powerful woman, a shark among the lesser predators feeding in the neltway, always promoting programs and ideas that Portia detested, wanted to discuss with her. Tureen was at her well-groomed best, making Portia feel as shabby as the room they occupied. That added to the misery of her nausea. A wary and troubled Portia was on her guard, her senses as sharp as she could make them. She sat on a metal chair close to Tureen.

"Well, Portia…. May I call you Portia? I think the question is probably what we can do for each other. For once, it seems, our positions on an issue are aligned. I'm talking about the parks bill."

"Aligned? I thought you were supporting the bill vigorously."

"Yes, but there has been a change of heart among my betters."

"Your betters?"

Tureen chortled. "That's what we call our clients. Sorry, it's an inside joke. Meant to be knowingly sarcastic. Last thing they are, of course."

"Of course.... Please say more about this alignment thing."

"Portia, let me provide a bit of background. In 2012, a number of western states, led by Utah, demanded that the federal government transfer to the states millions of acres of land, which, not to put too fine a point on it, is owned by the taxpayers. We argued that the states are better equipped to manage the West's natural wonders—better than the Forest Service, BLM, and other national land management agencies. After all, those lands are within the states' boundaries, and we all know how badly the national government manages things."

Portia bristled at this observation.

"I challenge that premise, unless you mean 'Congress' when you say 'government.'"

Tureen smiled her patented friendly but condescending smile.

"To continue, we delayed going after the national parks and wanted to work on the issue incrementally. Get control of things like national forests and grasslands first, and then springboard to real jewels like Lake Powell and the Flaming Gorge National Recreation area. Once the states managed to establish 'ownership' of those areas, we felt comfortable in addressing the transfer to the states of the national parks."

"I see," said Portia. "But, catch me up. I don't recall any such transfers happening."

"You need to add 'yet,' dear. It's true that that aspect of state's rights is a little touchy for tree huggers, environmentalists, and their ilk, but we were making headway. Just look at how we managed to revoke the rules about logging roads and clear-cutting in public lands. It's a good beginning."

Portia began to understand the conflict that brought Tureen to her office.

"So, the plan to sell the parks to the highest bidders forestalls your clients' intention to acquire the parks for nothing, and sell them off themselves, right? You need to challenge the act to preserve the parks for your clients' predatory interests."

"You are sharp, dear. You've summed it up nicely."

Portia felt her gorge rising, and she was not sure whether the nausea was another visitation from her future child or a visceral response to her visitor's hypocrisy, to the outrageous suggestion that they had similar interests.

Portia calmed herself and reached for one of the Eternalchill® water bottles by the table, pouring herself a mouthful, playing with the cold water in her mouth until her nausea receded. Tureen gave her a solicitous look.

"They say that pot is helpful in overcoming morning sickness," Tureen offered. "I just refreshed my supply—if that would help. It's in the new packaging that dissolves under the tongue. The BestBuzz Raspberry mint flavor, I believe."

Portia politely answered, "Thanks, but the water seems to have done the trick. Let's talk more about our 'aligned interests.'"

As Tureen went into detail about the ways in which they might coordinate their efforts to derail the Parks Act, Portia was trying to balance on the horns of her dilemma. Unquestionably, the support of Tureen and her firm would improve the odds of defeating the act. However, were they successful, Tureen's next step would be to lobby for the national parks to be turned over to the states. Portia recalled John Muir's position on that...*really bad* idea.

Smiling, she focused on Tureen. "What you suggest makes a lot of sense, and your help would be invaluable. Let me pass this by our executive board and I will get back to you right away." As a signal of impending trust, Tureen beamed her most private number to Portia's fob.

The receptionist eagerly escorted Tureen to the office exit as she glided past gray cubicles housing overworked tree huggers, pipeline rejecters, greenies, enviroterrorists, peaceniks, and other riffraff.

Out of the office, Tureen escaped to the comfort of her exquisitely restored antique Hummer and told her man to drive slowly by the mall so she could re-establish her feeling of self-worth by viewing the government buildings where she and the money she marshaled reigned supreme.

The insistent bleat of her fob distracted her, and she pointed it at the beige partition behind her driver where the image of Benjamin Franklin Chang quickly materialized.

Chang, one of her more important clients, was born in Hong Kong, educated in public schools and Cambridge in England, and returned to Hong Kong to head the family business after his father met his premature death at the hands of assassins hired by unreasonable competitors. The family businesses branched into ocean freight, investment properties in Macau and Hong Kong, heavy construction equipment, prostitution, extortion, and drugs, mainly cheap opium derivatives.

As seen in bright three dimensions on the seat in front of her, he was standing near a railing overlooking the outer harbor of Macau.

"Hey, beautiful, you look terrific, as always. Just wanted to check in and also let you take a peek at my new boat."

Chang adjusted the lens on his fob to panoramic view and displayed an enormous cream-colored vessel. His transmission lingered on the helipad, Olympic pool, and amphitheater, the harbor glistening in the background. Tureen could not tell how high it was, but it was certainly the largest private ship she had ever seen. She turned slightly, showing off her best semi-profile, and said, "Looks fabulous, Ben. Had it long?"

"Just pulled into port last week. The ship came from Oman and was called the *Al Said*, which was the name of the sultan there—egotistical bastard. So, I bought it at auction last month after the sultan ran out of money. The reason he ran out of money is (hehehe) that he was killed in the battle of the Sultanates when the Sunni and Shi'a invaded for the oil reserves and then decided they couldn't get along. Another bloody Middle Eastern mess."

Tureen appeared to listen attentively as Chang continued to show off the features of his newest acquisition and offer sage pronouncements about how he was profiting from the "Middle Eastern mess." Meanwhile, her brain was clicking through possible answers to Chang's expected question about the Parks Act, rationalizing ways to reconcile the diametrically opposed desires of the western states governors she represented and billionaire Chang.

"And I acquired not only the yacht but also some prime real estate with water in Oman. Be worth a lot someday. And, of course, they were worried that the boat would be destroyed by the Shi'a just to piss off the Sunnis, so they quickly delivered the boat here at no extra cost."

Tureen watched Chang rub a white powder inside his cheek, cough, and move his prominent nose closer to the fob.

"So, the other thing is that I've been following what's happening with the Parks Act, and it looks like good news all around. Out of committee in the House and up for a vote in the next few weeks. Beautiful! You're doing a great job."

Tureen shivered involuntarily as he said "beautiful." He licked his lips and leered suggestively at the same time, making his tongue appear like the glistening head of a piranha as it protruded toward her from the seat back. Damn this enhanced 3D, she thought. It can be frightening.

"So," he added, "just wanted to touch base and tell you that I have changed my interest from the Everglades to the Smokies. Turns out that my plan to cut a channel across the lower half of the state was already tried by the Corps of Engineers and, national park or no park, there was too much flak about turning the lower half of the state into an island. And then, of course, there's that problem with southern Florida soon being under the ocean because the dyke system isn't working right.

"There's a lot more land in the Smokies anyway, and the minerals and timber there are fabulous—to say nothing about the potential for more amusements parks like Dollywood and BrooksPark. And, just between you and me, I am working to push through laws to permit bordellos in parts of Tennessee. Why should Nevada and New Mexico be the only states that allow wholesome adult entertainment?"

More white powder disappeared inside Chang's cheek.

"OK? We OK with the Smokies? Give me a quick update. How long is it going to be before we can get serious about making a bid? I have my guys all set up in Atlanta as US citizens."

Tureen flashed her most ravishing smile at the seat; its wattage could cut through tungsten.

"Ben, I've got it. We will continue to pursue your and our interests with everything we can muster. If there's a God in Heaven, you will be king of the Smoky Mountains in less than a year."

"That's just what I need to hear, gorgeous."

His hand moved toward his fob, jostling it slightly, exposing two voluptuous, bikini bottom-clad Asian women next to his chair. To Tureen's relief, he deactivated his fob and the seat back returned to light beige—with no protuberances.

Tureen had found a nicely evasive response to Chang's question. As far as she was concerned, there was no God. Consequently, her false assurance to Chang had a ring of optimism and truth, two commodities she rationed very closely.

She sank back into the ebony recesses of the Hummer. In her most private thoughts, she considered Chang a disgusting, overeducated, criminal slimeball. On the other hand, he never challenged her invoices, never balked when she raised her hourly fee to fifteen hundred new dollars, never put a virtual hand on her. Of course, they had never actually met in person, all contact having been by 3D fobcast. Slimeball or no, he was a revered client, deserving of her best efforts. It bothered her that Chang was putting her into a position where she had to deal with a conflict of interest.

She reflected, however, that even her best efforts to influence legislation occasionally failed.

Representing the corn industry the previous year, she lobbied to increase the congressionally mandated percentage of ethanol in gasoline from ten to twenty percent. In the face of rapidly reducing gasoline use, that would sustain the annual volume of corn used to produce heavily subsidized ethanol. The unpalatable alternative was to export corn at lower prices to starving citizens of third world countries. Unfortunately, Tureen was unable to suppress the AAA study that cited reduced fuel efficiency and "the potential to cause catastrophic engine damage." AAA also pointed out that older vehicles would unquestionably experience poor drivability and reduced engine reliability. The ethanol measure died an orphan's death.

Even though she salvaged some business by lobbying for the delivery of corn to clients in sub-Saharan Africa, the ethanol failure stung. Yet, Chang had to be aware that she was fallible, that even she might "drop the ball before the finish line," in one of the hackneyed sports metaphors used in the capital. She could always ruefully recall such an instance of failure if he challenged her efforts on behalf of the Parks Act. She was now committed to the cabal of governors trying to divert the nation's land patrimony into their own boundaries and hands.

She sank more deeply into the soft leather interior of the Hummer, enjoying the parade of brightly lit national monuments as dusk descended.

It's going to be a win-win, she thought. However the Parks Act turns out, one client will be happy, and the other can be mollified. She released a contented sigh, and then flashed back at Portia Merson, poor thing, pregnant and fighting a losing battle at the National Green Defense League. Tureen resisted a feeling of maternal involvement.

THE TENTH FLUSH

Reluctantly, Portia filled her glass from a bottle of sparkling water. She felt, on the one hand, noble and selfless for honoring her pregnancy and the health of her embryo by avoiding alcohol and, on the other, annoyed that she could not relieve the daily stress of her job with a soothing glass or two of wine. Although she had told Grover that it was "just fine" for him to indulge in mild alcoholic intake, he seemed to be enjoying his glass of cabernet sauvignon too much. She secretly wished she could rescind her previously granted permission to imbibe. It would be unfair to Grover. Nevertheless, Portia was in a grumpy mood. She sipped her water and cleared her throat.

"Um, I saw Doctor Hasty this afternoon," she said." She reviewed junior's human germline—you know, the map of his genome. It was very interesting."

Grover sat up straight, fully at attention. The wine glass was on the coffee table.

"You never mentioned that this morning. What's the news?"

"I didn't want to concern you until I had something to report. It's all good," she said.

"All good? Junior is fine?"

"As good as a four-month pre-emergent baby can be. Well, there is one little thing," she added.

"A little thing?"

"You remember we talked about Wylie getting a bit forgetful and how his memory was improving with those dementia praecox pills?"

"Sure," Grover said worriedly.

"Well, Dr. Hasty read out the synopsis of junior's genome analysis and it all points to him being a very healthy, intelligent person. But he does show a tendency toward early onset dementia on that genome. There are choices we can make at this point."

Grover thought he understood what that meant, but asked Portia to explain.

"It's pretty simple. Dr. Hasty can edit the DNA using the Crispr-Cas9 method. You know, where they alter the natural immune system to attack genetic invaders when they appear. Or, since it is only a probability, we could just wait and see if the disease actually occurs and treat it with medicine. I am leaning toward using the 'Crisper' method. Get it over with," she said.

Grover searched his memory. There was something about editing DNA that he recalled, and it bothered him.

"Wasn't there a problem right after the FDA approved the Crisper method? Something about sloppy editing and babies coming out with extra ears, fingers, and toes? And how the cure for Down syndrome gave people vestigial tails?" Grover asked.

"Oh, the method has improved a lot since then. The DNA editing nowadays is extremely precise, according to Dr. Hasty. The risk of cutting off the wrong part of the genome is minimal."

"Screw that!" he said. "Not to argue with you, Porrie, but I would rather wait and see, and then fix any problems that might arise later. I am not willing to take the risk that some butterfingers might mess up my son's genome. Let's wait, OK?"

Portia saw his point. Medications to cure diseases, except the virulent airborne virus mutations that reliably killed millions each year, were constantly improving.

She moved toward Grover on the couch and sat close.

"Agreed. We'll wait and see how junior turns out."

Tureen was skilled at keeping in mind the truths, half-truths, and outright fabrications she used to mollify her various clients. Keeping those on opposite sides of the same issue happy and motivated was one of the great talents that helped her rise to such prominence as a Washington lobbyist. It was not easy work. In addition to remembering a tangled skein of stories, she had to make sure that there was no fraternization among opposing clients. Fortunately, she conducted most of her meetings by 3D fob, and when physical materials, like outmoded cash or actually minted bitcoins, needed to change hands, she employed services like ExpresDrones®. Therefore, Benjamin Franklin Chang's opening statement when she answered her fob disturbed her.

"Listen, gorgeous," he said, licking his thin lips and acting as though he could see through her clothing, "I have had a severe reversal of fortune, and need to discuss an urgent and delicate matter with you. It is possible that I can meet with you in a day or so, if I take the orbital flight to DC."

"Ben, as always, a pleasure to hear from you. I hope everything is all right," she said, noting his red-rimmed eyes with accompanying bags. Meanwhile, her mind was racing to find a way to avoid his coming to her office. Many of her clients favoring the death of the Parks Act were visiting during the next few days.

"No, everything is not all right," he responded. "In fact, everything is a monstrous cock-up. I am, as you Yanks say, up shit's creek without a paddle."

She could see that Chang was sitting in front of his office window, which displayed the broad expanse of the Hong Kong harbor. In the near distance were three dockside warehouses emblazoned with the logos of Chang's companies. In front of one warehouse was the cream-colored bow of a large vessel protruding from the dark green water like the head of a gray whale, pointing directly skyward.

Chang turned to snort something, wiped his nose, and continued.

"Three days ago my yacht was docked over there," he said as he pointed to the cream-colored bow adjacent to his warehouse, "and I was enjoying the company of a number of good friends on the ship. Apparently, one of my friends used a below-deck head and, when she flushed it, it triggered a massive explosion that ripped out the bottom of the ship. Poor girl was never seen again and the rest of us barely managed to reach the dock before the ship sank, stern first, and settled on the bottom of the harbor."

Tureen was properly aghast.

"How horrible! How did it happen?"

"Salvage divers examined the entire ship during the last thirty-six hours and discovered triggering devices attached to some of the toilets rigged to detonate explosives hidden along the hull. When any one of those toilets reached its tenth flush—ka-boom! It was done with easily modified mini-fobs concealed in the flushing mechanisms."

"How horrible!" Tureen repeated. "Who could have organized such a thing?"

"Well, there are plenty of business competitors here and there who would like me out of the way, but all the recovered explosive and triggering parts point to Oman. A couple of my vice presidents already reviewed the matter with the seller in Muscat who, unfortunately, suffered a heart attack right after the meeting. He confirmed that local Shi'a functionaries might have tinkered with the ship before it left port in Muscat."

An assistant leaned into the scene, whispered in his ear, and showed him some information on a Quick-tab®.

"Ahah! There it is. Confirmation. My people have found and dispatched the parties involved in Muscat. Unfortunately, their demise will in no way compensate me for the terrible loss I have suffered. I am a victim here! The supposedly first-class maritime firm insuring the boat was a sham, and all my premiums went to support the Sunni factions in the ongoing war of the Sultanates—after the defeat of the Caliphate. To make matters worse, all the instability in the region has made my oceanfront properties there almost worthless."

Tureen was sympathetic to her client's misfortune.

"How can I help?" she asked.

"Obviously my priorities have changed. Let's put the Parks Act on the back burner. I need you to get Congress to bail me out and make me whole again. That's the least they can do considering how much I paid to keep many of them in office. Right now, gorgeous, I'm out over eight hundred million dollars. You need to slip that amount into the appropriations bill for the TRA (Terrorism

Relief Act) to recompense me for my losses at the hands of an acknowledged terrorist organization."

"Well, that's a tiny amount to add to the bill and shouldn't be a problem," noted Tureen, "but remember that compensation can be made only to United States citizens."

"Yes, I almost forgot that. So, get me on that expedited naturalization path right now and I can get the terrorism relief in a few more months. That would work, wouldn't it?"

Tureen looked dubious.

"Listen, Ben, no one looks carefully at your background when you are handing them money, but it's a whole other thing when you buck the line to get citizenship. There are all those indictments, rumors about criminal business practices, the girls who claim you sold them into slavery..."

Chang looked both weary and irritated.

"Let me remind you, gorgeous, I have no convictions."

"Of course, that's in your favor. I am sure that will resonate with my contacts in the legislature."

Chang reached toward his fob, indicating their discussion was ending.

"We are clear, are we not? You will work to arrange my financial relief and I'll wait until that is settled before becoming the Sultan of the Smokies."

Chang offered a mirthless grin. Tureen returned a practiced smile.

"Yes, I know. That is so. I am not a miracle worker but, as always, I will do my best."

With a hint of menace, Chang broke off their talk.

"Just so, gorgeous; your best has always been more than enough."

As he faded from view, Chang seemed to be staring at Tureen's nipples. She hurried to the office bathroom, peeling off her clothes. A long shower and some good whiskey might make her feel clean again.

Sneath Naydir was beginning to mix up his Susans.

His infatuation with "Susan" derived from his first sexual encounter, which was with young Susan Entlich, a robust farm girl from Minot, North Dakota. The encounter occurred in the hayloft of her family barn where she and Sneath retired after observing the family bull demonstrate his prowess at procreation. In the hazy sunlit afternoon the size and efficiency of the bull's pizzle intimidated Sneath, causing him to feel puny and inadequate by comparison. Susan, however, focused on the cow, feeling rising excitement and a glowing in her loins. She suggested that she and Sneath inspect her newly hatched chicks in the barn.

There she quickly offered her unclothed body for additional inspection, causing Sheath to shed his feelings of inadequacy and satisfy both their hormone-driven desires. Like a baby bird imprinting on the first object it sees, Sneath associated his glorious sensation of release with Susan, and that name evoked a sense of comfort and satisfaction ever after. The original Susan matriculated from a teachers college after their summer of romance, married a farrier, and operated a very successful cattle-breeding business.

Now, there were four Susans in Sneath's immediate circle of people designated as "contacts" by his fob.

First was his wife, nee Susan Smatterwaithe, the mother of their two children, with whom Sneath performed the husbandly obligations needful to maintain a blissful suburban household. Sneath called her "Susanne," embellishing her name for additional luster.

Next was Susan Spraddle, office and bedmate referred to as "Susie," a playful companion, willing lover, and efficient assistant who helped manage his business engagements and all aspects of his personal affairs. Those included a willingness to indulge Sneath in some of his curious extramarital requirements that were to cause him future difficulties.

"Suz" was a recent hire and up-and-coming office assistant on track to become a junior partner in their lobbying firm. She was efficient and well endowed intellectually and physically, qualities Sneath respected and enjoyed. He saw her both as an asset to their business and a potential replacement for Susan Spraddle should she become unavailable because of marriage or a better job offer. Suz was unaware of Sneath's designs on her.

Susan Armitage was Freddie Naydir's fifth grade teacher. Freddie was a mildly autistic student who could do sums in his head faster than a math fob. Sneath and Susanne met with Freddie's teacher often to review their son's progress at mainstreaming in a class appropriate for his age. Ms. Armitage, as Sneath referred to this Susan, was a tall, willowy blond woman with aquiline features; helpful, friendly, and bright.

Sneath decided to incorporate her into one of his many sexual daydreams. A recurring and most pleasing image of Ms. Armitage appeared. She bent over him, wearing a flimsy teddy, high black leather boots over mesh stockings that exposed her toes, and red earmuffs. She wiggled her toes and poked him aggressively with a leather-tasseled riding crop.

The warm-hearted and compliant Susie Spraddle graciously indulged Sneath in some odd fetishes. She tolerated his licking and sucking her toes as she played solitaire on her fob. She actually enjoyed his slurping Drambuie from her navel, but was confused when he requested she feed him chicken noodle soup with a baby spoon. Nevertheless, she complied. Susie did balk, however, at riding him bareback as he cantered about their hotel room.

Sneath, therefore, was accustomed to enjoying some of his harmless fantasies. Where he had difficulty was in remembering which Susan satisfied the particular desire of the moment. On the day before his meeting in Senator Hinckle's office, his inability to manage Susans caused a family crisis.

When he returned late in the evening to his home in Bethesda, he was happily inebriated. A late dinner with Frank Crouch at a favorite watering hole involved consumption of cocktails, wine, and excellent port. The Selfer® asked him to repeat his home address twice before landing at his doorstep.

Even his racket when entering his home did not wake Susanne, who had fallen asleep to the latest reality program that required unarmed contestants to survive late-night walks through the South Side of Chicago. Her clogs had slipped off so Sneath saw her bare feet exposed and protruding at the end of the couch. He could not resist. He kneeled on the floor next to his wife, cradled one foot gently in his hand, placed his lips carefully over the top of one big toe, and sucked the toe with an ardor that threatened to dislodge her toenail.

For a moment or two, it was pure bliss. Then Susanne awoke. She looked down at her feet.

"Ick! Ooooh! Ick! Ick!"

She yanked her foot away, producing a sound like a popping wine cork. The force of her withdrawal pulled Sneath's head forward onto the glass coffee table by the couch, on which he cut his lip and narrowly avoided the destruction of two capped teeth.

Now fully awake, aware, and shocked at Sneath's behavior, she demanded an explanation. Why on earth was he sucking her toe? What kind of pervert was he?

Trying to explain the unexplainable, Sneath propelled a splatter of blood from his cut lip on to the cream damask couch. That was enough for Susanne. She ran to their bedroom and locked the door. Sneath collapsed into the floor, shuddered once, and began a dark dream where a fire-breathing dragon wearing red earmuffs chased him across the Aerotica landscape.

The next morning Susanne refused to speak with him. He began the day with a swollen lip, sullen wife, and cold coffee.

DISTURBANCES

S neath thought he had taken the correct detour to reach the Senate Office Building, but he alighted from his Selfer® too close to the place where a crowd was forming. One of the daily legally sanctioned angry crowds of protesters, usually marching against social inequality, financial inequality, underfunded practices of sexual deviation, war, or poverty, was milling around police barricades protecting the Ulysses S. Grant Memorial. The picketers carried signs demanding "Save Iowa" and "Nebraska—Never too Late!" referring to legislative inaction in resolving the years' long drought in the Midwest. Ranchers, dairy workers, farmers, cowboys and many of their working robots moved along Maryland Avenue toward the Capitol. The crowd seemed well behaved, but Sneath knew that pent-up anger sometimes resulted in violence toward passersby, especially well fed, well-dressed, and legislatorly-looking people. In hopes of exploiting entertaining violence, members of the media had plugged in to surveillance viewers that monitored the area.

A tall, slender man in faded blue jeans wearing a weather-beaten straw hat addressed the crowd through the megaphone attachment on his fob.

"How long? How long do we have to eat dust and watch out kids starve? How long? How long will we allow the fat assed legislators sucking at our government's tit to ignore us, to demean us, to force us from our homes?"

Rage quickly stirred the crowd. The protestors pushed forward toward the Capitol, toward the barricades, toward the location Sneath thought to be safe. Nearby, one of the protesters made a menacing movement toward a young policewoman, who immediately directed a warning arrestor beam to his chest. He backed away, noticed Sneath, the picture of sartorial and gastronomical excess, and moved toward this less threatening quarry. Sneath unarmed but for a fob, proved that discretion is the better part of valor. As the large man moved in his direction, he walked away rapidly, down the block toward the next cross street. Distracted by the arrival of a team of snappers (android dogs with extremely large jaws and teeth) the man lost interest in Sneath and looked to his own security.

Safely around the corner, Sneath paused, out of breath, grabbing his knees, sucking gobbets of air into his lungs. Crap, he thought, Susie was right. He had to lay off the pepperoni, the donuts, and the expensive scotch. Hit the gym. Yeah, hit the gym. Recovering his breath, he straightened up and walked slowly toward the building where he could ride the subway to the chamber. He adjusted his tie and moved forward on the path of good intentions that led straight to Hell.

Ron Snecker, the senate aide to the 4-H club, kept him waiting for more than twenty minutes. He wore a look of contrition as he wove his way to Sneath and offered a pasty hand. He gave a listless greeting of "Howyadoon, buddy?" and motioned for Sneath to follow him to a small conference room near Senator Hatchett's office.

They sat near each other and, in an effort to delay the inevitable, Ron offered Sneath a NicoTame® cylinder, which Sneath refused. He had given up tobacco years ago, though he still worked for clients who demanded that tobacco remain an uncontrolled substance, even though everyone seemed to know that tobacco products killed a half million Americans a year. Undisturbed by that statistic, Ron placed the cylinder between his lips, pressed the orange start button, and vaped the heated purified nicotine vapor into his lungs, feeling almost instant contentment. It would make his conversation with Sneath easier.

"So, Sneath, the thing is that I don't think we can count on Porter Hinckle's support of the Parks Act. He's had a change of heart. Something to do with letting the buffalo range free, protecting the environment, that sort of shit. I don't know what else to tell you; Porter's mind is made up. It came as a real shock to all of us. You know, being a staunch member of the 4-H Club and all."

Ron held out both hands, palms up, in a gesture of disbelief and frustration. It took a few moments for Sneath to absorb this unwelcome news. Suddenly, he felt as winded as he did after running from the menacing crowd. He leaned toward Ron with a puzzled look reddened by rising anger.

"How the hell can this be? Just a few days ago, Hinckle was a strong advocate for the Parks Act. If he withdraws support now it could destroy all our work to assure a supermajority in favor. Some in the other party might waver! This is a disaster!"

Ron replied that he was fully aware of the political fallout of Hinckle's reversal, not the least of which would be expulsion from the 4-H Club and loss of some privileges. Sneath probed for information about what might have influenced this sudden interest in "doing the right thing." Ron ransacked the cupboard of his memory; a crumb fell out.

"Well, funny thing was, Hinckle had his assistant call over to the National Green Defense League to announce his change of position. Never had anything to do with them before. Gimme a sec, I'll check."

Ron touched one of the tiny buttons on his fob, scrolled to the recording of that conversation, converted it to text, and projected the readout for Sneath. The assistant's message resided in Portia Merson's input log.

"Yeah," said Ron. "I met her when I worked over in the House. Pretty, smart girl. Tilting at windmills, but savvy. You know her?"

"Heard of her," said Sneath, as indeed he had. She had successfully blocked some of his other initiatives during the past few years.

"So, I guess I need to find out whether this Portia is involved in Senator Hinckle's sudden decision to thwart the Parks Act," said Sneath.

Unlike some of his other assignments where dollar signs were merely in the hundreds of millions or billions, the passage of the Parks Act easily involved trillions upon trillions of new dollars. That was real money; it could assure great personal wealth for Sneath. He took a threat to the Parks Act personally and seriously.

"Just so you know, I checked all our logs for the past few months," said Ron. "Portia Merson hasn't visited our offices or called in over two years."

"Then I will just have to look into this another way," confirmed Sheath as he prepared to leave. Ron seemed very relaxed, his eyelids drooping slightly, his handshake more flaccid than before. Must have added some of that Cannibest® to his e-cig, thought Sneath. He almost regretted the work he had done to legalize pot in all fifty-one states. There were just too damn many happy but unreliable workers in the district. Turned Ron into a pussy. Have to find a more reliable cohort in this office.

Sneath left the subway and decided to walk partway to his office—to enjoy the soft spring afternoon and begin his exercise program. He considered the Portia Merson question. The signals that she was involved in the defection of Senator Hinckle seemed clear. In fact, the senator may have intended to convey that message by openly contacting her. A reasonable person, who Sneath considered himself to be, could fairly conclude that Portia represented a sincere threat. To be dealt with.

He felt a pleasant tingle along the back of his neck as he pondered an appropriate way to discredit—no, destroy, her. He, however, could not risk being directly involved in that process. His furrowed brow smoothed as he recalled the perfect person to help, as she had done times before. No fingerprints. No regrets. He couldn't wait to return to his office to contact his former ally, the beautiful, formidable Tureen O'Porto.

The cuff of his DigiShirt® pulsed. He glanced at the reportal there and saw the subtle warning outlined in strands of glowing thread: *Elevated Blood Pressure. Mild Tumescence.*

Senator Deborah Hatchett glared at Porter Hinckle sitting on the other side of her desk, his attempt to look nonchalant ruined by the nervous twitching of his right leg. They both knew their conversation was being recorded, which Hinckle hoped might tone down the tongue-lashing he expected. He peered up at the senior senator and saw no compassion, no forgiveness. Had he miscalculated? Was she actually prepared to disclose that he was a closet pederast? No, he thought, not old Deb. I've got a lot on her, too.

She began. "Listen, you peckerhead asshole, I don't know what kind of crap you're pulling here, but it looks to me like you have made a life-altering decision by removing your support of the Parks Act. This is now personal with me. It's a simple matter of whether we can trust you. I need to know, right now, that you will come to your senses and support us. Otherwise..." She leaned forward ominously. "...you will find yourself in a shitstorm of hurt."

Hinckle cleared the lump in his throat and pressed a hand down on his unruly right leg.

"Come on, Deb," he began. "It can't make that much of a difference. The act has solid support and the loss of one vote won't matter one way or the other. There are strong personal reasons why I can't support the bill anymore."

"Personal reasons? Bullshit! What personal reasons? Like they say, it's either money or sex. Your penchant for little girls and boys biting you in the ass?"

The blood drained from Hinckle's face. His wide-eyed stare confirmed to Senator Hatchett that this open secret about Hinckle's ill-disguised predilections lay at the root of the current issue. Her face softened.

"Listen, Porter, if that's the problem, there are ways we can deal with it. Even if it's a journalist or a parent. As you know, everyone has secrets. I've been here a long time and I have never seen intimidation or lots of money fail. Hell, that's what our discretionary budget is for!"

His sudden relief quickly evaporated. He could not imagine a multi-millionaire like Melvin Salmon influenced by money or intimidated by people whose own secrets he controlled. The risk of grasping at Senator Hatchett's straw was too great. He would nobly stand his ground and avoid being outed by Salmon.

"Thanks, Deb. I honor your experience and help, but this is something the usual practices won't fix. I just can't change my position. You don't know how sorry I am."

Senator Hatchett looked at the wet-eyed Hinckle, this sad sack of a senator, and decided further attempts to change his mind, while potentially enjoyable, would be fruitless. As for revenge, she expected that the consequences of this decision would fuel Hinckle's many future sorrows.

"OK, Porter, you can consider yourself retired from the 4-H Club. We have a couple of qualified candidates to take your place—and your office. You will no longer retain your current committee assignments. I will work with the leader to move you to the Sewage and Sanitation and Military Condolences committees. That will free you up to spend more time dialing for dollars since I don't think our reelection committee members will be passing much money your way. As time goes on, I feel sure we will find other privileges to retire. Now that I think of it, don't plan to join us in the Senate dining room."

Senator Hatchett puffed her cheeks and expelled wind past rubbery lips, a sign of terminal dismissal. Porter Hinckle gathered himself and tried to straighten his shoulders as he left her office. The loss of this powerful friend was stingingly apparent when he turned the corner to his office and saw that a worker was unscrewing his walnut name plaque beside the door.

As Wylie promised Portia, he kept in touch with Senator Rowe to glean information about the mood of the senators and changes in individual leanings toward or away from support of the Parks Act. As lobbying intensified from all sides, he noted a shift among moderate senators against the act, while those on the left and right hardened their positions. Particularly adamant were those on the far right who were convinced that facts had a liberal bias and were therefore untrustworthy. Their obsidian obstinacy in favor of the Parks Act continued.

Senators leaning left as though buffeted by a strong nor'easter had a more favorable view of facts, but they ignored unfortunate truths, believing that high-decibel recitations of favored facts would drown out unpleasant reality. Although they did not influence other senators to change their positions, they formed a bloc of unshakable votes against the Parks Act.

Wylie, with Senator Rowe's help, shared with Portia and Tureen O'Porto that there were twenty-seven unchangeable votes for the Parks Act and twenty-three against. Thus, fifty-two senators might be swayed one way or the other. The two women clearly understood their challenge: thirty-nine more votes against the Parks Act would deny its proponents a supermajority, and the act would not pass.

"Let's just shoot for an even forty votes," suggested Tureen. "I like living on the edge but I am getting to a place where I want the margin for error to be on my side."

"Works for me," said Portia, ignoring her sinking feeling as she considered the enormity of that task.

The more experienced Tureen also recognized their challenge as she considered various ways to influence the senators. In the back of her mind was her recent conversation with Sneath Naydir soliciting her help in "destroying that Portia Merson bitch." Obviously, he was unaware they were working together and were well on their way to forming a permanent friendship. As she turned the irony of the situation over in her mind, she searched for a way to thwart Sneath **and** use that as a way to enhance their lobbying efforts. Wouldn't that be delicious!

After two months or so of procedural delays, senators began to debate the merits of the Parks Act before airborne S-Span 3D cameras. Meanwhile, Portia and Tureen encouraged determined members of numerous environmental and economic groups to mount public awareness campaigns throughout the country. Since the legislation had passed the House with only a slim margin, efforts to secure senators' votes intensified. Former presidents, the Clintons and Obamas, argued in favor of keeping the parks under the control of taxpayers. Aides to the assassinated President Ryan put aside their grief to promote diminished government, and fiscal responsibility.

The ailing Reverend Al, just released from federal prison in Danbury, Connecticut, for tax fraud, rallied his troops and led numerous marches to save the parks. His supporters provided a gold-plated golf cart that he used in leading marchers through major cities near national parks.

Celebrities expressed their opinions in many ways. Yancy Farker, the country western singer, joined opera singer Fredonia Amalfi to sing his latest hit, "Park It Here, Mama." Ken Burns reissued his television series about the national parks, updated to include heartfelt endorsements from current Hollywood luminaries. Clint Eastwood, almost one hundred years old, sent money, a 3DVD of his latest movie, and two pistols to Senator Hazard. A conclave of Native American tribes paraded through many of the parks in vintage attire, performing ancient rituals and dances as park rangers tried to enforce the rule against topless dancing.

The debates in the Senate, interspersed with scenes from the national parks, played nightly on nationwide television. Talking heads on Fox News expanded their arsenal of misinformation, and talking heads on PBS valiantly tried not to put the audience to sleep. Polls showed the nation evenly divided on the issue, forty-five percent for and against the Parks Act, and ten percent wishing the pollsters would go away and stop bothering them.

A Pew survey showed that the polls really did not matter, since Congress had been ignoring them for years. Many members of that august body continued to sponsor or suppress legislation claiming they were following the will of the American people even though polls showed the exact opposite. Self-delusion in the Capitol rose to new heights. Nevertheless, polltakers continued providing unheeded information.

MODERN
TECHNOLOGY

Now at the end of her second trimester, Portia was developing a slight potbelly, hardly noticeable on her tall frame. Morning sickness was over, and she enjoyed a strong feeling of well-being, joyful at impending motherhood. Grover shared that joy, received as by osmosis from Portia. The absence of irrational mood swings helped, and he teased her about cravings for unusual foods like pickles, herring, and Cherry Garcia ice cream. The prospective Madonna was calm and cheerful, in spite of the pressures of her job and discouraging lack of inroads toward defeat of the Parks Act. Friends remarked how wonderful she looked.

"My, you look wonderful," said Tureen as Portia eased herself into Tureen's office on K Street. It was Portia's turn to visit Tureen's office. Tureen found it difficult to be creative in the shabby conference room of the National Green Defense League.

Portia hefted her messenger bag onto the conference table and settled in the chair by Tureen's desk, and Tureen's assistant offered tea and pastries. Portia laughed.

"I would love tea, especially English breakfast if it's available. But, that harridan who calls herself my obstetrician says now is the time for willpower if I want to retain my girlish figure 'after the event.' Just pass the pastry dish under my nose so I can enjoy it vicariously."

Tureen, blessed with a metabolism that seemed to turn cakes, pastries, and cookies into rock-hard muscle, helped herself to a blueberry scone and passed a spreadsheet to her friend.

"You don't need to read it; exactly the same as last week. My assistant collated the information from your grandfather, Senator Rowe, Grover's people, and our own sources. Even if we turn the 'undecided' votes against the Parks Act we still come up short. A number of delaying tactics remain under the new Senate rules, but we have only a couple of months before a vote is finally taken."

Relying on recent Harvard Medical School studies of in vitro sensibilities, Portia tamed her first impulse to utter an appropriate curse like a simple "shit" or the half-word "mother." She did not intend that her son could someday claim that his use of foul language derived from her cursing during pregnancy. She mouthed an appropriate obscenity to Tureen, who nodded approvingly.

"Positions are hardening," said Tureen." I think that if the vote were held today the act would be on the president's desk tomorrow. Somehow we have to find a new and dramatic way to turn this around."

The specter of doom settled over the conference table as the two bright women rehashed, reconsidered, speculated, and engaged in flights of fancy—to no avail.

Tureen said, "OK, let's put a pin in it for now. There are a couple of new items I want to get on the table."

Anything, thought Portia, to dispel the current gloom. She looked at her belly. Was nourishing this future man-child sucking away her creative juices? It was a frightening thought.

"You know the smarmy lobbyist who made his bones by pushing tobacco and pot, Sneath Naydir?"

"The pudgy guy with the single eyebrow?"

"That's him."

"I hate to admit it," said Tureen, "but, in times past, we worked together on a couple projects. He developed an attraction for me, which I definitely did not reciprocate. Anyway, he contacted me and the subject of conversation was you."

"Me?"

"Swear to God."

"Me?"

"Wants to mess you up, though he didn't use that exact term. More like 'destroy her ass' and 'get her out of the way.'"

"Me!"

"Like I'm telling you. He was raving about how you turned Senator Hinckle against the Parks Act, that he was sick and tired of your getting in his way, and somebody needed to teach you a lesson."

"I had no idea," said Portia. "Anyway, I didn't have anything to do with that. Out of the blue, I got a call from his office, letting me know that the senator was going to oppose the act. I was very surprised because I had given up lobbying any of the 4-H Club senators. This is very odd. I should check it out."

Tureen reexamined her conversation with Sneath in light of Portia's information.

"Portia, leave that for the time being. Let me look into it from here. I have a contact in Hinckle's office." A wicked twinkle appeared in Tureen's eye. "Meanwhile, let me fill you in on how we might use Sneath's request to our advantage."

Tureen reviewed potential ways to deal with Sneath as Portia listened, wide-eyed, at her friend's devious and near-criminal scenarios.

"I'm not sure I could approve any of those ideas—they are so complicated. Please, let me think about it a bit more," said Portia.

"Of course," said Tureen, secretly excited at the prospect of orchestrating a complicated scam against a fellow lobbyist she considered less honorable than pond scum. "There is no rush about this; it is all just conjecture anyway."

Portia did not feel assured by Tureen's offhand dismissal. From recent experience, she knew that her friend would examine every angle of a new idea like a jeweler counting facets of a diamond. She would categorize the thought, check it for flaws, and, if acceptable, place it on a bright setting in an accessible corner of her intellect, ready to recall as needed.

There was a moment of silence as the two women exchanged wary smiles.

Portia said, "So, what was the other thing we needed to talk about?"

"Right! The thing is that the only national parks I ever visited are the Mall and Lincoln's and Jefferson's memorials. Since we've been working together, I have to confess that I feel my own experience may be too limited to be an effective advocate. Yeah, I know I talk a good game, but I feel a little guilty for never actually having visited an important national park."

Portia affected a joking tone, even though she was impressed that Tureen might want to enjoy an outdoor experience. "You telling me you might be getting hooked on nature? Hard to believe from such an effete sophisticate as you. You could break a fingernail, and I don't think Prada carries hiking boots. However, tell me more."

The teasing continued.

"Oh, sure. This from a woman who barfed twice when we walked a half mile on the Appalachian Trail."

"Not fair! It was morning sickness."

"You're right. I take it back. What I want to tell you is that my client, the governor of Arizona, has invited me to do a three-day rafting trip on the Colorado River through the Grand Canyon. I am excited about that and, since I have no 'significant other' at the moment I was hoping you and Grover might come along."

Now, this is unexpected, thought Portia. First, she found it difficult to believe that her beautiful friend had no current romantic involvement. Her guess was that a squad of potential suitors was at her disposal. Second, as exciting as a trip on the Colorado might be, she thought it ill advised to risk her pregnancy on the exertion of maneuvering a raft on a swiftly flowing river. She and Grover had rafted the New River the summer before, accepting the challenge of coursing through number five rapids and frequent dunking as the raft fought its way through eddies, reversals, and hydraulics. No, rafting would have to wait until her man-child made his debut.

As though anticipating the thought, Tureen said, "I wasn't thinking you and Grover would do the river; you could enjoy the views from the rim while I rafted, and we could see the sights for a couple days after. We have two suites available at El Tovar, which I hear is a lovely lodge. Come on, we could use a break from this incestuous pest hole."

Under those conditions, Portia was sure Grover would join them.

Sneath was exhausted from explaining to his clients why there was no action on the Parks Act. No one was interested in the arcane rules that the Senate made up for itself in the absence of direction in the Constitution. There was, for example, no cogent reason that passage of some measures required a simple majority while others demanded a supermajority of sixty-two votes. The newly elected leader of the Senate risked losing her position if she chose to revert to a simple majority to pass all legislation, as many scholars believed the founders intended. Only more experienced clients like Frank Crouch understood these irrational niceties; he called mainly to assure himself that Sneath could guarantee enough votes to pass the Parks Act. He was concerned about the defection of Porter Hinckle from the 4-H Club, and would tolerate no more surprises.

"Frank, it's safe as houses," Sneath told him. "We count noses day and night and there are sixty-five votes for the act. Sure, we lost a few along the way, like we expected, but this is solid. We just have to be patient while they play all those procedural games. Come July/August the act will be on the president's desk—and you know where he stands. Eager would be an understatement."

Frank Crouch knew nothing was ever "safe as houses." He recalled all the assurances Crouch Industries received about how the battle of the Sultanates in Saudi Arabia and Oman was a tempest in a teapot, and that there was no possible way it could affect their Middle Eastern interests. Then the battling factions overran the Arabian Peninsula and shut down or destroyed billions of dollars of Crouch infrastructure.

We spent almost as much on our own army of mercenaries, he thought, before we stabilized the area, but we lost a fortune. In the end, they were unable to save dear friend Al Said, the Sultan of Oman, from that unfortunate interaction with a scimitar. He still grimaced at the Sunni joke: Al(l) Said and Done.

Crouch decided not to challenge Sneath's cheery assessment of the political situation.

"Just so you know, Sneath, our attorneys are standing by and ready to file numerous bids for desirable parks before the ink from the president's pen dries. Our focus remains on the Grand Canyon. By the way, how are you coming along in lobbying the secretary of the Interior, the Ferrari guy? We could use some clout there."

In a massive understatement Sneath said, "He is stepping back from the details of the bidding, but we are making inroads with the Parks Department people involved. They are the ones who count."

In fact, Agatha Jackson had signed placards reading, "No [expletive deleted] Lobbyists Allowed within 100 yards of my office. Those who ignore this will be Violated." She taped them along the corridors of her office building. The only inroads people in his firm were making were along those leading to the Department of the Interior.

"Good to know," said Frank Crouch. "Sounds like you've got it covered."

Yet, there was something in Sneath's delivery that was vaguely disturbing. Well, he thought, all this unnecessary waiting has us all on edge.

Sneath adjusted his fob to receive Tureen's call. Alluring as ever, she explained that she was responding to his inquiry about Portia and suggested they meet privately, in the open, to discuss the matter further. They selected the sidewalk on Constitution Avenue across from the First Middle Eastern War Memorial.

Tureen kept Sneath at arm's length as they met that evening during rush hour, when vehicle lights brightened dusky shadows. Passersby would have wondered about the tall, lovely woman speaking so earnestly to the nondescript man in a too-long coat.

"What we do, Sneath, is turn off our fobs and hand them to each other. But first, my fob will check you for other devices."

"Seems a little unfriendly," offered Sneath, but then handed over his fob.

They walked slowly along the broad sidewalk toward the Capitol, intrigued by the recently installed billboard over the entrance that counted the number of days Congress had been in session that year, a reaction to the groundswell of public irritation at how much the legislators paid themselves for the few days they actually were in session. Now that holographic appearances at their desks counted, the public seemed mollified with the higher numbers.

"What you may not know, Sneath, is that Portia Merson and I are working together on a project I am not at liberty to discuss. I see her frequently and am familiar with her habits. I even warned her that the scuttlebutt said you intended to harm her. Of course, she scoffed at that. Sneath, Portia does not seem to hold you in high regard."

"Bitch!" he exclaimed.

"No matter," Tureen went on. "Having considered ways in which to destroy her, I concluded that fabricating a story about her infidelity wouldn't do the trick, since that is all too common. Offering phony confirmation that she was involved in running an escort service is out, too. That's just old news, making it to just page 20 in the *Post* and lasting less than ten seconds on Twitter or Nipster feeds. Unless there is blood or exposed genitalia, Fox won't cover it. Even *Congressional Diarez* wouldn't be interested."

Sneath became testy.

"I don't need you to tell me what won't work," he offered. "How about what will?"

"Drugs," said Tureen.

"Drugs?" asked Sneath.

"Specifically, selling highly purified Fairoin® to grade school kids."

"Damn," said Sneath, "that's a title three controlled substance. As I recall, dealing gets years in the U.S. Antarctic penal colony, you know, the successor to Gitmo. That's hot, Tureen!"

She outlined the plan. She would place an illegal amount of Fairoin® (more than six ounces) in the trunk of Portia's Prius along with forged thank you notes from sixth graders in the Capitol Gardens Country Day School. Syringes, hot taps, and other drug paraphernalia would be concealed in a robin's egg blue Tiffany box to suggest she was not only a drug dealer but also an effete, well-heeled Eastern establishment drug dealer. Naturally, Portia's DNA would be found on all these articles. If her two broken taillights did not attract the attention of the Capitol's finest, an anonymous z-mail would.

"You certainly don't take half measures," offered Sneath. "I am in awe of your creativity! When do you think you could complete this, um, project."

"I think I could manage it sometime next week. There is just one detail I need your help with aside, of course, from your maintaining absolute discretion and secrecy about the 'project.'"

"What can I do? What can I do?"

"It's not as though I have Fairoin® on the condiments shelf in my kitchen. Those days are long over. Since I intend to involve myself directly in making this happen, I need your special help."

"Sure. Whatever."

"I need you to pick up the Fairoin® from one of my old contacts and, to make sure you have skin in this game, pay for it as well."

"Sure. Pay for it. No problem," said Sneath, trying to avoid making the last phrase sound like a question. Spending his own money always made him queasy. Certainly, this would qualify as a deductible business expense. He brightened.

"So, what should it run, moneywise, I mean?"

Tureen was motioning to her driver sitting in her idling Hummer.

"Oh, offhand I guess a couple thousand bitcoins. These guys are not gougers. I'll give you the address this week. You can set it up."

Sneath waved good-bye to his partner in crime as the glistening antique Hummer pulled to the curb and the door opened for her. She waved back over her shoulder.

As part of his new program for physical self-improvement, Sneath decided to return to his office on foot, his pace hampered slightly by his SpanxX© body electro-shaper underwear, designed to take off pounds effortlessly. He paced his stride to the gait suggested by his underwear and soon enjoyed the balmy evening and the feeling that he and his underwear were one, a feeling, he expected, that was like riding a favorite horse. Unfortunately, as an early adopter, he had purchased the 1.0 version of the new underwear, which, like most new products these days, was expected to fail no more than fifteen percent of the time.

As Sneath paused for a light before crossing Constitution Avenue, he experienced a warm, tingling sensation behind his scrotum. It was quite pleasant at first, perhaps an undisclosed design feature from the creators. By the time he crossed the avenue, however, that area began to take on Saharan proportions. He made it half a block before he had to stand, spread legged, by the curb trying to catch breezes from passing cars and busses.

As he stood, his testicles expanding from the unaccustomed heat, he noticed the hot spot between his legs cooling slightly and began to think about his dilemma more rationally.

The sales clerk, he recalled, explained that both his body heat and his movements powered the electro-shaper, the way the energy from a braking car made electricity. Maybe, he thought, there was some kind of a short circuit down there and when I move faster, it makes it hotter. Following that assumption, he ambled twenty yards while monitoring the burning fork of his legs. It seemed to get no worse; no, wait, it did!

Back to the curb. Hoping for busses with their abundant gusts of smelly but cooling air, he tried to feel for the micro button controlling his underwear. It was not where it should be! Apparently, that was the defect; the control button had caught a seam on his shirttail and fell away, lodging at the top of his right sock. There he was, legs akimbo, stretching against the mystery fibers of his underwear, wishing he could open his fly, vainly poking around the top of his sock, searching for the elusive micro button.

"You got a problem, sir?" asked the young Asian police officer who peered down at him, a look of sincere concern on her face.

"Omygod! Omygod!" moaned Sneath, resisting no longer, forgetting the button, ripping open his fly, sinking to his knees on the curb. A large bus flew by, nearly rocking him off his knees. She steadied him and asked a simple question,

"You got one of those 'lectroshapers on?"

"Yes," he managed to say.

She continued to support him as her Bodycom® system recorded Sneath's gyrations, and spoke with a superior.

"Got another dog with hot pants here. Second one this shift. Send a bus, and I'll get him away from the curb."

She helped Sneath across the sidewalk to a low wall and pulled a blue plastic pouch from her side pack, pulling a tab that caused the materials inside to react. She applied the cold pack to the affected area, causing instant relief.

She smiled. "How about modern technology! I been carrying these cold packs ever since those 'lectroshapers came out. Don't feel bad. Looks like you had it mild. There have been a few with second-degree burns. Just hang in there. The bus will be here in a minute."

Sneath was having dark thoughts about modern technology.

THE CANDY DESK

"There was something Sneath said that gave me pause," Tureen told Portia. "Remember, he seemed to think you were responsible for changing Senator Hinckle's vote on the Parks Act although you had nothing to do with it? That bears investigating, and I have a good contact over in the senator's former office. Check your z-mail and tell me exactly what day you received that note from Hinckle."

Portia did as asked, and Tureen expertly manipulated her fob, which soon projected the image of a middle-aged, pleasant-looking blond woman sitting at a wooden desk in a large office space. Tureen adjusted the fob so Portia was not visible to the woman.

"Oh, Tureen, it is so nice to see you!" the woman said. "I feel guilty that I haven't thanked you yet for the lovely fruit basket you sent to our room at the hotel you recommended in Miami Beach. You were right about the flooding, too. We stayed in the reconstructed area with the walled-in beach and had a wonderful time. Those new water taxies got us to the mainland in less than ten minutes."

Like two puppies wagging their tails in greeting, the conversation meandered on, until Tureen revealed the purpose of her call.

"Gladys, I wonder if you could check into something for me? I am looking into something that might be helpful to Senator Hinckle..."

"Oh, the poor man," said Gladys. "He was moved out of here in a New York minute; hardly had a chance to say good-bye…"

Tureen cut in. "Yes, I know. It's a shame…"

"Crying shame!" added Gladys.

"Right. But here's the thing, I wonder if anything unusual might have happened in his office on April fourteenth. You know, extra-long meeting, strange visitor, unexpected absence—that sort of thing."

"Well, I don't know. I'll have to look." Gladys referred to another screen on her desk, humming a popular song about termites slightly off key. Suddenly a surprised look followed by a grimace of distaste crossed her placid face.

"Oh, right. That scruffy man with no sense of politeness showed up that day. He talked to the senator, but I know the senator didn't like him. When he left, I saw Senator Hinckle throw his business card into what he called the 'burn box'—you know, the autoclave shredder. That man, he was not what I would call a nice person, you know?"

Tureen said she knew.

"So, Gladys, were the usual images of this man collected?"

"Don't you know it! Holographic, too. We have this new storage module—keeps twenty-four hour records for eight years. So small it fits into a space the size of one of those little Fiats…"

"Amazing," said Tureen, biting her thumbnail to restrain herself from screaming at Gladys. "Tell me, Gladys, could you pull up one of those images so I could take a peek?"

"No problem. I just gotta review the protocol because I don't get to do this very often."

Gladys pressed some keys and examined her desktop monitor. The termite tune returned as she concentrated on the monitor and tried pressing a few more keys.

"Shoot," she exclaimed, blushing deeply. "I thought they had cleaned out all the porno on the Senate network. Keeps coming back like mushrooms after a rain."

After two more failed attempts, Gladys squealed triumphantly "There he is!" as a detailed image of Melvin Salmon, scruffy beard and all, popped from the screen.

"Got it," announced Tureen as she grabbed the image. "Gladys, thank you so much."

"No problem, Tureen—any time," said Gladys as her image fluttered and disappeared.

Tureen repositioned her fob and projected the very lifelike image of Salmon for Portia to view. At first, she did not recognize him, as he was heavier and hairier than when she defended him, but then she identified him.

"Will you look at that? It's Mel Salmon; I know him from a while ago, when he was still in college. He was a pro bono client. Brilliant kid—just a little twisted. He created that avatar game company. Worth a bundle, I think. I haven't seen him in years."

What, wondered Tureen, did this media mogul want with Senator Hinckle? Was there a connection between him and the senator's change of position on the Parks Act? Was there a remote chance that Mel Salmon was a secret ally? So many questions. She asked those questions of Portia, who also drew a blank. Portia and Tureen penciled in a meeting with Mel Salmon on their shrinking to-do list.

Less than a third of enfranchised Americans cast their ballots during the most recent midterm election. Some analysts claimed the majority of voters had succumbed to terminal disgust with the legislature, believing it made no difference whether they voted or not. Others developed an ostrich theory, suggesting that voters simply ignored proceedings at the Capitol, kept their heads down, and hoped for the best. One pundit hoped that a powerful hurricane encouraged by rapid climate change would create a massive tidal bore in the Potomac and inundate the Capitol along with its unruly inhabitants.

Others, mainly legislators, chose to believe that the American people were so content with the status quo that it was not necessary for them to make their voices heard. In any event, impassioned pleas in favor of or against the Parks Act were embraced so long as they supported the legislator's heartfelt position. Otherwise, legislators ignored such pleas, considering them ignorant.

Yet, doughty senators, by habit or conviction, continued to debate the vital issues encompassed by the Parks Act for about a half hour every other workday as the act glided snail-like toward cloture.

"This is a balancing act, the thing we were elected to perform on behalf of the American people, the purpose of which was enumerated by our founding fathers, the kind of hard decision we came to Washington for," said Senator Hatchett during her time allotted to defend the Parks Act. "There is no pro or con here. We need to support the pros, which we are bold to follow. And I plan to explain them again today, if I may." She paused to let her oratory sink in among those in attendance in the chamber, somewhat put off by the glistening, opaque figures of the senators attending by hologram.

She sipped from a glass that appeared to contain water, glancing at the list of assigned speakers. "Frosty" Sommers, speaking in person from across the aisle, came next. He was the junior senator from Louisiana with a Cajun accent so thick that S-Span's closed captioning was required to follow his rambling trains of thought, thoughts as peculiar as "his houn'dawg Blue searchin' for fleas near the part where the sun don't shine."

She well knew Frosty was against the act primarily because of his love of open spaces and distrust of private interests that frequently befouled his state's delicate coastline. He seemed immune to the excellent financial arguments explaining the benefits that would accrue to the country as a whole by the efficient disposal of an underused and costly asset. It was like dealing with one of her large affordable-housing units in a rundown area when the nuisance of providing heat, working plumbing, security, and drinkable water became bothersome. Sell it and move on. Simple. She felt frustrated that this senator from an adjoining state refused to listen to reason. She adjusted her next comments to parry Frosty's anticipated statement.

"There are some who say we are abandoning a national asset because we have mismanaged our economy and are desperately searching for a way out," she said. "That is so far from the truth it is laughable. Laughable. To accuse the legislature of mismanaging our economy displays ignorance of founding principles of separation of branches of government. It is our responsibility to provide funding, and the executive must wisely use those funds to make our economy work. Consequently, and with deference to the current occupant of the White House, if our economy is in outhouse mode, do not look to the legislature. We are doing our job."

Frosty, believing Senator Hatchett had made her point, rose to rebut her. However, she was just warming to her task.

"In fact, by proposing this action, we are offering a responsible way out of our current dilemma—at no cost to the American taxpayer. We will convert the current value of the parks, well known to the American people as an underused asset since they are populated mainly during months when children are not in school, to funding for critical national needs! And those needs are enumerated on the 'c-chip' previously submitted to the leader for dissemination in the chamber—so I will not be exhausted in their enumeration."

Senator Hatchett paused to take another sip from her glass.

"Frenkly…frankly, I little doubt that, under the auspices of good management by the business people who will manage the, uh, parks henceforth, we will see a great improvement in their use, management wise. Look at how… Just look at how insurance companies managed the rollout of the drug provisions of Madicare…Medicare. After just four years, they reduced our drug costs to 255 percent of what Canadians pay. There are other examples wish you know about that I refuse to bother you with at this point in time. That having been said, I respectfully take my seat."

Triumphantly, she lowered herself to the yielding cushion of her leather chair.

Senator Sommers took the podium and thanked his good friend for her lucid comments. "However," he added, "much of what you just heard amounts to not a bit more than a pile of horse pucky."

Then the senator went on to disparage each one of her points in colorful terms, taking full advantage of his constitutional right to absolute freedom of speech in the chamber, without threat of litigation for libel, slander, cursing, or flamboyant lies. Consequently, when the senator began referring to "animal lovers" in connection with the parks, his listeners were unsure whether he was referring to a deviant sexual practice. He was almost at the end of his allotted time, speaking of the endangered albino alligators in his beloved bayous, when Senator Smart, Republican from the great state of Vermont, rose to ask Frosty to yield.

"And why should I yield?"

"I rise to address the chamber about an important housekeeping issue that just come to my attention," said Smart.

"Housekeeping issue that's more important than the Parks Act?"

"Perhaps. It involves the candy desk."

Ah, the candy desk, thought Sommers. An honored institution of the Senate, beloved by all. In a tradition begun in 1968, Senator and former movie star George Murphy kept a drawer full of candy at his desk located near an entrance to the chamber. Although Senate rules prohibit eating in the chamber, members of the body gratefully received those sweet tokens for, presumably, later consumption. By tradition, the candy desk was stocked by its current occupant.

Sommers yielded, and Smart informed the chamber that "since the terrible drone accident that took the life of our beloved Senator Palin, who occupied the candy desk until her recent demise, no one has been assigned to stock the candy desk. Until her replacement is designated, there will be an unacceptable lack of candy for this august body. I propose measures be taken to remedy this breach of a great Senate tradition."

A murmur of concern rippled through the chamber. An astute listener would have heard whispers of Skittles, M&M's, Mars Bars, Hershey's Kisses, Milky Ways, Jelly Belly, and Mike and Ike. Concern mixed with relief. Critical as the Parks Act was, the debate was taxing both the patience and intellect of some members. Respite from the knotty issues of the act was welcome. As though illuminated by a flash of lightning, the chamber brightened. Suddenly, senators seemed eager to join the candy debate.

Smart plucked strings of nostalgia.

"Who does not recall those years ago when my dear friend Rick Santorum from the powerful state of Pennsylvania occupied that desk? Ah, the Hershey's chocolates and Just Born candies that he supplied so generously, those delectable products from his home state.... Who could forget the two-pound silver

Kisses stacked by his desk on Valentine's Day? Or the Hot Tamales that heated us up on a frosty Washington morning? Is there anything more…"

The presiding officer, afraid that Smart might be launching one of his stem-winders, interrupted.

"Senator, do you have a proposal?"

"Indubitably! I think we should assess each senator a small fee to be contributed to a candy fund, administered by a designee of the president pro tem."

Rumbling engulfed the chamber. Not Senator Rumbling from Arkansas, but a palpable snarky murmur audible to all. Was Smart suggesting they invade their personal funds to support a hitherto cost-free perquisite of office? Bipartisan disagreement about his suggestion arose almost immediately. Heads shook, fists clenched, knowing glances were exchanged. Regional and party differences evaporated in uncommon unity.

The presiding officer said, "We shall take your excellent suggestion under advisement; consider it tabled for the moment. Do you have anything to add, Senator?"

Before Smart could reply, Tom Claghorn, the tall, bushy-headed senator from Oregon, interrupted, words fighting to slip past the white walrus mustache he favored.

"Speaking for us members on the other side of the aisle, I wish to recall Senator Smart's attention to the candy desk visible to all in the rolltop desk located on the front wall. Though the desk and its contents belong to the Democratic Conference secretary, I know I can say without fear of contradiction that, in the best spirit of bicameralism, we would be honored to share the sugary contents of that desk with those on the right side of this chamber."

A chill fell on the right side of the chamber. The prospect of accepting **anything** offered from the opposing side was unthinkable.

Smart responded, "Generous as the offer from my friend from the great state of Oregon is, I cannot accept. It is my understanding that the Conference secretary's desk is filled with small caramels, stale licorice sticks, outdated toffee, and unclad Hershey's Kisses, hardly the fare suitable for the members on the right side of the aisle. I respectfully reassert my suggestion of establishing a candy fund for the entire chamber."

The trajectory of a small caramel remaining from a previous distribution from the candy desk interrupted the mild applause from the right. Coming seemingly out of nowhere, it crossed the aisle, passed harmlessly through a surprised holographic senator's image, and skidded across the top of Senator Smart's bald, slippery head. Quickly other missiles sequestered in senators' drawers and of questionable age and vintage changed Senate sides. Mars Bars fell on heads and shoulders. Skittles littered the aisles. Mr. Goodbars studded the thick carpet. Well-aimed tootsie rolls found soft targets.

The nearest sergeant-at-arms suffered from gout. She rushed as quickly as she could while pushing her walker to the edge of the melee. At the same time, visitors in the gallery recorded the scene below on their fobs, immediately broadcasting it to instant news outlets worldwide.

It was many minutes before the chaos ended. Sticky chocolate- and sugar-covered heads and hands were visible throughout the august chamber. Assistants rushed to actual senators in the chamber with damp towels and fresh makeup. Virtual senators, recognizing that their presence would no longer be needed, switched off. Their images shimmered in the disturbed air of the hall and became insubstantial, like fog dissolved by morning breezes. Sergeants-at-arms confiscated all visible potential missiles. The presiding officer brought down her gavel on the oak disk on her desk to end the session, not realizing a peanut butter truffle had fallen squarely on the disk. The session ended with a whimper, not a bang.

It would be three days before debate on the Parks Act resumed.

THE MARCH

Looking into the monitor, Agatha Jackson adjusted her park ranger tunic and campaign hat. Farnsworth Nuñez, her assistant, adjusted his fob to display the words of her speech clearly at a comfortable distance from her eyes, but not in view of the camera. Agatha felt a flutter in her stomach and suspected beads of perspiration were forming under the curly hair at her temples.

She knew that the twenty thousand people working at the national parks were deeply concerned about the Parks Act and thirsted for information, for her leadership. Though constrained by a prohibition against government employees involving themselves in politics, Agatha believed she retained her freedom of speech, regardless of how many government agencies monitored every outlet of communication under the recently renewed Loyalist Act. Bravely, she accepted the consequences of the inflammatory proposal she was about to announce to the dedicated members of her beloved agency.

Agatha intended to sponsor a day of civil disobedience, during which as many park employees as possible would leave their jobs and march in uniform on the Capitol, holding banners and signs proclaiming that the parks belonged to the people. She would ask relatives, friends, and lovers of the parks to join the marchers. Those who could not reach Washington would hold mini-marches within the parks, encouraging visitors to demand that their legislators reject the Parks Act.

Portia Merson and Tureen O'Porto encouraged this act of defiance, and helped organize transportation and logistics for this great event. Today, Agatha intended to confirm the rumors about the parks march and rally the people whose jobs depended on public ownership of this great national resource. It was the first time she had addressed all her people on a multi-fob hookup.

She did not take her responsibility lightly. A history enthusiast, she reviewed famous speeches from the past: Henry V at Agincourt; Eisenhower on D-Day; Churchill's we shall fight them on the beaches; Hillary Clinton's this shall not pass; Justin Bieber's fool that I are. From these sources, she created her speech. Now it was time. The red light on the camera glowed. She spoke to all the workers at her much-loved parks on the secure parks network.

"Thank you for joining me at a time when we are beset by confusion, irrationality, and fear for our livelihood," she began. "Within a few weeks, our legislators intend to decide whether the government should sell our wonderful parks to private companies or individuals—under conditions that do not promise their long-term use by our citizens. I am sure you feel, as I do, that this is a rash, unconscionable thing to do, penalizing all citizens for our government's inability to manage well our national assets, our economy, and our future. Others are on our side, but we cannot be silent, we cannot permit the wholesale loss of the most beautiful and fragile parts of our country. I call upon you to act!"

Agatha looked directly into the lens.

"On April 23rd, National Park Week begins. I ask you all to mark that date as the day of the national parks march, and join me in a march up the Mall to the Capitol to confront our legislators, to call them crazy and un-American, to tell them we want our parks back, to fight for our peaceful enjoyment of our land's God-given beauty.

"Some say we are too few, that we need more voices to be heard. I know we are strong and loud, that we are abundant, and that we will be sufficient. Those who fear the march, stay home. Our march will not be contaminated by the uncommitted.

"So, you and yours who believe in what is right, join us on that day. On future days when the great march on National Parks Day is recalled, you can show your park badge, you can tell your grandchildren that you were there. You will proudly let them know that you were one of the brave men and women who made your stand, who helped save the country from the ravages of unprincipled legislators.

"Mark your calendars. April 23rd will live as a day of distinction. Join us. March with us. You will become one of the happy few, the band of park rangers forever."

The unblinking eye of the lens stayed on her; then the red light faded. Suddenly her fob vibrated like a Cape Cod shutter in a nor'easter. A thousand voices clamored to be acknowledged, to offer congratulations, vent their hatred, offer threats, ask questions, seek directions. By priority, the name continually scrolling across the top of the fob was that of her superior, Noble Ferrari, secretary of the Interior. The warmth of her finger released his brief message: "See me urgently."

Amanda tossed her campaign hat on the chair by her desk, straightened her tunic, and walked the long corridors to Ferrari's office.

"He's waiting for you," chimed his assistant, pointing to the open door to the secretary's office. She entered, dazzled as always by his splendid collection of Native American artifacts displayed throughout the suite.

Ferrari sat behind his large walnut desk directly under a stuffed buffalo head, which complemented his burly face. He looked up from messages scrolling down his fob monitor and sighed, dropping his shoulders and puffing his cheeks. Agatha recognized that as a sign that he was about to convey a decision, a rare occurrence in her experience.

"So, Agatha, take a seat. Thanks for sending over the outline of your talk, which I probably should have reviewed more carefully before now. I liked the 'band of rangers' part. Had a nice ring to it. Sort of familiar, you know?"

"Thank you. It was…"

"Right. Thing is, I received seven tweets from very important people during the first thirty seconds of your talk, even before your 'crazy and un-American' legislators part. The mildest one recommended that I sack you immediately.

Others mentioned treason and a firing squad. It certainly has livened up my morning."

Agatha felt a prickly sensation on the back of her head, fear mixed with indignation. Her throat tightened. She knew her speech would be inflammatory and had prepared herself for the worst. Now, she believed, the worst, being dismissed from her beloved agency, was about to occur. She stiffened in her seat. There would be no apologies. She decided to interrupt.

"Sir, I know you have access to our secure communications channel, but how did very important people manage to listen to what I said?"

Ferrari seemed relieved to change the subject, even briefly.

"Oh, what level channel were you using?"

"Level A-8, the most secure one."

"Ah. That one's been hacked for days. It's such a bother. You must have missed the memo."

He clicked a key by his monitor and words tumbled across his desk.

"There it is.... Oh, I see the problem. Frances forgot to forward it. She must have ignored the 'need to know' bulletin. Government bureaucracy, right? Ho."

He offered her his patented sincere sheepdog look, so useful when he was an assistant attorney general, and decided to revert to the topic of her speech.

"You know, Agatha, a critical aspect of being a successful politician is avoiding controversial decisions. To that end, I have simply avoided making any decisions while in this office, permitting my subordinates to fulfill that function. So far, that approach has been successful, and I have been able to avoid any unpleasantness. Of course, a few underlings are no longer with us, but that's the way of the world, isn't it?"

Agatha slid forward on her chair, looking directly at Ferrari, hoping she would not cry when he next spoke.

"After your speech, which apparently has already gone viral, I must break precedent and respond directly, actually take a decision. I admit, I am annoyed that you have forced me to take a stand. However..." Here Ferrari hunched forward and smiled at Agatha. "...I will stand with you. You are on the right side of history. You are correct to try to save our parks. On every level—moral, practical, and ethical—I agree with you. I plan to tell all the very important people to go fuck themselves. That okay with you?"

At six in the morning, April 23 promised to be a perfect spring day—cloudless, still, not too warm. Pale pink blossoms embraced the ground beneath cherry trees and floated on the surfaces of reflecting pools and estuaries like wedding confetti. Busses from other states began to park on side streets to the Mall, rumbling diesels providing a resounding bass to the serious purpose of their passengers. Waves of police officers in deep blue, waves of guides in neon yellow and red T-shirts brandishing tablets, and waves of hawkers selling Smokey the Bear balloons and plastic campaign hats bore down on assembly points. First-time visitors looked in awe at the marble monuments glistening near the Mall, put off slightly by the splotches of red and orange defacing the Washington Monument.

Tureen reluctantly agreed with Portia to join the march for a mile or two. They arrived early to secure a place near the front of the line, less than a quarter mile from the Capitol. Portia was eager for relief from the frustrating work of pushing against immovable objects, and looked forward to walking on a fine spring day among like-minded people. Tureen arranged to have herself photographed among the marchers to prove her bona fides to her clients opposing the Parks Act.

Both women discovered many employees of the national parks already there. Rangers and police officers carried sidearms as required by law. Many civilians carrying Rugers, Colts, Glocks, Pumas, Remingtons, Magnums, and others of the scores of handguns manufactured in the United States joined them. These enthusiasts seized every opportunity to display their weapons under the recently passed NOCA (National Open Carry Act). They did not seem like fervent supporters of the Parks Act to Portia. She thought they looked like gun lovers taking their pets out for a walk.

Tureen noted that some civilians were beginning to line the curb along the route of the march. Some of them also carried pistols and signs. The signs were flagrant examples of the extremes of free speech, heavily larded with four-letter words and rude graphics depicting immoral and impossible acts between trees and people. Between the marchers and their hecklers stood a line of police officers determined to retain order as the swelling group of marchers shuffled in place, herded by volunteers holding bullhorns and whistles. Police control stations were set up at various street corners leading to the Capitol, and busloads of reserve officers waited quietly on side streets, not far from the busses that carried marchers to their destination. It was nine in the morning, half an hour before the march was to begin.

Sergeant Trudy Fenster looked down the street lined with trees displaying fresh green leaves, observing the crowd of marchers and the pedestrians testing police lines, stepping from the curb here and there.

To Patrolman Bensil Farnack she said, "Yeah. Fine spring day. Early yet. And here we are, babysitting another effing march. We had the million-man, the two-million-man, the half-million gay pride, the queers on parade, and now it's the tree huggers. And it looks like every third one of them is showing off a 9 millimeter or 37 Magnum. See that numnuts over there, the one with his belly overhanging the grip? How long you think it would take him to clear his holster? Pathetic. Yeah, pathetic!"

"You think those assholes on the hill regret passing NOCA? Christ, we need twice the people we had to control these dickheads on the street," offered Bensil.

"Doubt it, man. This march might get their attention, though. A lot of angry people are planning to charge the steps, I hear. They won't make it; even so, our action will be visible from their offices. We'll be ready with armored vehicles, stun guns, chopper dogs, ammonia water, and all that stuff. I just hope none of these trigger-happy buzz heads get out of line. You can't believe the paperwork when you retire one or two of them permanently."

Bensil nodded his head knowingly.

"Don't I know it? I got two weeks probation for tuning up one of those teenage dronie punks. Little bastard used his parents' printer to build the mini-drone parts, filled the cargo container with indelible pigment, and crashed it into the Washington Monument at 2 a.m. Real high. Up close to the top. You can make it out from here. Little bastard complained I broke his nose... little bastard."

Their conversation turned to other of their pet gripes, mainly about the futile task of helping clear buildings when another terror attack was anticipated or called in. Now, many people worked from home, conferred by satnet, or used hologram. There was reason to worry. The most recent successful attack was on the Supreme Court Building. Four pillars on its left side were under restoration. A Scottish-Armenian terror group, the MacKeranians, claimed responsibility and, so far, had eluded all efforts to locate and destroy them.

The officers' conversation halted when the numnuts Trudy had pointed out before drew his weapon, fearing an attack from a passing Pomeranian on a ruby leash. Trudy rushed toward the numnuts to thwart a potential slaughter.

All this was observed and recorded on the ubiquitous button cams located every fifty feet or so throughout the Capitol. Images of daily activity streamed wirelessly to an undisclosed location deep in Catoctin Mountain, where a multibillion-dollar array of compulizers reviewed the digital information, alerting human supervisors of anomalies. Lack of funding, however, slowed the process so that evidence of offenses was reported days after the event. Managers disguised the failure of the system by calling it "protracted sequential lagging," a term no one else understood.

Arriving early rewarded Portia and Tureen with a place close to the beginning of the march and a few yards from the place where a ubiquitous black MUV (metropolitan utility vehicle) halted to deposit Agatha Jackson and a handful of broad-shouldered park rangers near the beginning of the column. The chief of heraldry of the Interior Department confirmed her civilian position was equivalent to a major general and supplied her with a set of two stars that gleamed on the epaulets of her ranger tunic. An aide directed her to the front of the column, now packed with her supporters as far back as the Lincoln Memorial. As she took her place, Agatha noticed Portia a few yards away.

Soon one of the rangers stood beside Portia, asking if she would like to join the parks' leader. Of course she would! How about her associate, Tureen O'Porto? The ranger mumbled into his hand; Agatha nodded her head and gestured for them to join her. Numerous nearby petty functionaries scowled and drummed their tablets at this unscripted breach of protocol. They thought better, however, of challenging the large, armed rangers surrounding their leader.

Or, for that matter, the over two thousand rangers and four hundred park police dispersed throughout the restive crowd.

"Oh, Agatha," gushed Portia, "your speech was so wonderful, so bold. You are a hero to all of us supporting the parks."

"Thanks, Portia," said Agatha, who then glanced at Tureen. "Ms. O'Porto, I didn't expect to see you here. Change of heart?"

"You might say that, Director. My heart belongs to my clients, who do not support the act. Portia and I are colleagues when it comes to maintaining the status of the parks. And, please know, I was moved by your speech to the rangers. Such eloquence and passions are rare in this town."

The sudden noise of whistles, bullhorns, a multitude of shuffling feet, and excited voices signaled the start of the march. The crowd moved forward with glacial majesty, led by a phalanx of three women—one pregnant, one black, one gorgeous—surrounded by park rangers and reporters wielding minicams recording their movements in 3D, 8G, and Tru-Audio.

Portia was thrilled to be next to her dedicated friend, encouraged by the large numbers of parks supporters, flushed by her emotions and deviant hormones connected to her pregnancy. She felt strong, empowered, and surprisingly happy. Her face glowed.

Tureen was happy to be in the vanguard of the great march, especially since the gaggle of reporters surrounding them seemed to be focusing frequently on her. Having her photogenic image seen on national and international news was an unexpected boon. Such exposure would certainly help justify her ever-increasing hourly rate. She did regret, however, wearing her Jimmy Choo pumps. Walking on asphalt was clearly not a task considered by Jimmy's designers, and it was difficult to smile for the cameras when her feet felt as though submerged in lava pools.

Agatha, approaching the Capitol, which gleamed under the bright sun as though lit from within, saw the navy blue ranks of Capitol police arrayed along the Capitol steps. Most appeared to carry stun blasters, tangle nets, chemoforcers, and other non-lethal persuaders, although some on the top steps carried dangerous-looking machine rifles and grenades. Their message and attitude were clear: no one gets up these steps or into the legislature. It seemed to Agatha a rather audacious and unnecessary show of force against a group of marchers intent on a peaceful demonstration. Why, she wondered, does the Congress so fear "we the people"?

The director of the national parks began to feel uneasy as the group moved along Pennsylvania Avenue. Her exhilaration at seeing the large gathering, finding Portia there, and feeling the support of those around her was fading. Replacing it was a sense of foreboding, encouraged by the various weapons brandished on all sides. My God, she worried, please don't let this get out of hand. As they reached the steps to the Capitol she felt relieved; just a few more yards to go.

Planners for the march did not notice that the Army's Presidential Salute Battery would practice its weekly drill at Arlington Cemetery that morning. Even at a distance of three miles, the cannon fire from Arlington across the Potomac River was impressive. The loud and repeated reports rolling across the Mall to Pennsylvania Avenue sounded like nearby thunder, causing some of the marchers to search for dark clouds in the deep blue sky. Some gun-toting bystanders squinted about for a possible enemy, hoping to stand their ground. Swiftly, bullhorns announced there was no danger, the Capitol police adopted a less belligerent stance, and people began to holster drawn weapons.

In the process, the national statistic of daily injuries caused by improper holstering of handguns rose by nine. Numnuts shot off his pinky toe; a ricochet severed two inches from the Pomeranian's tail; stray bullets nicked three testicles and one large female breast; and four foot injuries required medical attention. The participants reassembled as the wounded hobbled away, and the group slowly moved the last few hundred yards to the end of the route. The marchers spread out along the plaza in front of the Capitol, pressing forward against the base of the two long rows of steps leading to the entrance. Facing them was a formidable phalanx of police.

Aides informed Agatha of the injuries incurred, and she felt blessed that matters were no worse. Other marches had ended badly. The melee that occurred when the Daughters of the American Revolution attacked the Capitol police with knitting needles to preserve the right to bare their arms came to mind.

Agatha now stood on the lowest of the Capitol steps, Portia and Tureen at her side, a group of rangers around her preparing to move upward, a large and dedicated crowd of followers chanting now familiar slogans. Twenty feet above, helmeted police officers locked arms to block access. Her face was fixed in a look of bold determination. She glanced at the two women beside her, equally resolute.

"Anyone interested in a touch of civil disobedience?" Agatha asked. They smiled and all started up the steps.

Tureen was excited and pleased with her arrest. Unlike Portia and Agatha, who had developed a certain familiarity with police stations in their flamboyant youth, Tureen had never been inside a cell before. The experience thrilled her, made her feel ever so briefly like one of the downtrodden, the real people. She wondered if she would have a record. What an enchanting thing to mention at cocktail parties and client meetings. A thrilling chill went down her spine at the thought that others might consider her a "common person." How novel.

Portia reached Wylie on her fob even before the police pushed her into the back of a wire-screened electric bus along with Agatha, Tureen, and assorted demonstrators. He had observed coverage of the march on the taxi monitor as he rode from the airport for a lunch date with Senator Rowe. He saw the arrests made, but did not recognize any of those detained on the small screen. Consequently, Wylie quickly understood Portia's call for help, assured her he would handle the arrest, and called a promising young associate at Biddle and Ostrofsky's DC office.

Agatha's stay in the DC police station was brief.

"Geez, General, what in hell are you doing here?" asked the desk sergeant, a former parks police officer who immediately recognized Agatha.

"Lemme see," he said, examining the report on his fob, "'resisting arrest, disrespect of an officer, inciting to riot, failure to move on.' Looks like this patrolwoman swallowed a dictionary. I watched the march on our display panel and think I understand how she got confused."

The sergeant moved from his desk to a row of chairs, asking Agatha to join him. As they sat, he looked upward, as though stretching his brain to recall exactly what he had seen.

"General, what I recall is that you seemed to be pushed forward by the crowd and stumbled on one of the steps. You steadied yourself and your elbow caught the chin of the officer trying to help you. Your right arm went out and accidentally struck the officer on her chest. Happens all the time in crowd control. Total misunderstanding. Is that how you remember it?"

It wasn't, but Agatha readily agreed.

"Just want to let you know," he added, "that me and the missus and our two kids camp out in the Shenandoah National Park for ten days every summer. You keep it up; you keep the parks for us. And forget about the arrest. The recording got lost."

The sergeant shook her hand warmly and motioned her toward the entrance, past Portia and Tureen, who were waiting their turns.

"I am with these two women," she said.

Just as the sergeant began to review their records, Wylie and Sam Bankroft, experienced in the ways of the local police and courts, arrived. Portia ran to Wylie and hugged him, told him how much she appreciated his help. Tureen smiled at the old man, and Sam marched up to the sergeant's desk, clearing his throat.

The sergeant held up a hand and looked aside, then fixed the young lawyer with a weary gaze.

"Counselor, get ready for a big win. These ladies are all free to leave. We don't have room for them and it looks like they've had enough excitement for one day. Good day, ladies."

"Wait," Tureen blurted out, "you mean I'm not arrested?"

Surprised, the sergeant said, "Technically, yes, but by the divine intervention of Sergeant Xavier Kelly the arrest was annulled. It has evaporated. Poof. It is no more."

"Xavier Kelly?"

The sergeant gave a little nod.

"At your service, dear lady."

Portia took Tureen's arm and led her to the door, where Agatha, Wylie, and Sam waited.

"Mr. Cypher," said Agatha, "I understand you are helping us. There is a nice bistro not far from here. Would you and your associate join us for dinner?"

That is how the day of the "Save the Parks" march ended. A few arrests, some wounded participants, a sense of accomplishment.

The nighttime hush of the city seemed to swallow up all memories of the event. In a world where attention spans were measured in minutes and seconds, where each next big thing overwhelmed cascades of crises following one upon the other, the fleeting images of the marchers' conflict with local police receded from memory. The next day, on the hill, it was as though it never happened. Portia, Tureen, and Agatha gathered their resources to shoulder the boulder of the Parks Act, trying to move it in their direction. Agatha's speech, however, burned in the consciousness of the marchers and all those who loved the parks. It was not forgotten, and figured significantly, when, years later, Agatha announced her candidacy for president of the United States.

TOES AND THE TOKAMAK GENERATOR

Since the parks march and her brush with incarceration, Tureen noticed an unexpected change in her attitude about the national parks. It was as though she had found faith in something, as though saving the parks was important to her in ways other than purely financial. It was thrilling and troubling. She discussed it with Portia as her friend unfurled a mat to perform pregnant mother yoga exercises on the deep pile carpet in Tureen's office.

"So, I've been bothered about this strange feeling I have developed about my mission," she said.

"You have a mission?" asked Portia. "I thought you were the quintessential non-confrontational observer who acted as a hired gun for the highest bidder. It seemed like your mission was to make more than enough money to support your lavish lifestyle. How is that a bother?"

"Well, there is that, of course, but I was thinking about the Parks Act and how, after the march and all, I was actually feeling good about supporting the parks. Like it is a very worthwhile thing to do."

Tureen grimaced as Portia achieved a lotus position that balanced her embryo-filled belly on her calves, presenting an unflattering Buddha-like image of a pretty Portia's face on a bulbous body. Tureen vowed internally never to look like that…ever.

The Portia-Buddha spoke.

"It may be an unfamiliar concept for you, but have you considered that you might be developing a conscience?"

As the Portia-Buddha shifted from one asana to another, moving her body into positions that made Tureen uncomfortable just to observe, she considered that possibility. Since the march, Tureen felt a kinship with the other marchers, a sense that she belonged to a significant movement. As she created various media pieces denigrating the Parks Act, she realized that she was becoming passionate about the message, not simply feigning enthusiasm for the benefit of her clients.

Tureen watched Portia lick a bead of sweat from the corner of her mouth. She found it funny and endearing. She reflected on the strong friendship developed with Portia during four months of close association. Portia certainly did not offer unconditional support; they argued frequently and loudly. What, then, was the unusual, unexpected ingredient in their relationship? Tureen retrieved a towel from Portia's bag and handed it to her. Portia offered a grateful smile, and Tureen suddenly understood. Portia was absolutely honest and trustworthy. That was a new experience for Tureen. It was unsettling.

She returned to Portia's "conscience" comment and passed it off as a joke.

"Conscience? What on earth could I do with a conscience? That would suggest I have scruples or principles. No one can afford to indulge in those luxuries in DC. No, I plan to remain unconscionable."

Portia laughed at the word play and took a seat by Tureen's antique Hepplewhite partners' desk. She reconstituted a chilled bottle of water from her Thermobag® and reviewed the meeting agenda with Tureen.

"I see you contacted Melvin Salmon, my former client, now multimillionaire. How did that go?" she asked.

Tureen glanced at notes on her fob.

"Well, Melvin was surprised that I knew he had something to do with Hinckle's defection from the 4-H Club. Also, he was very interested to learn you and I are working together to defeat the act. When I told him you might be interested in a meeting to review common interests, he lapped it up like a cat on spilled cream."

"Hmm," offered Portia, "that's a bit strange. I haven't even seen him in over seven years. However, I would like to understand his interest in all of this. Have you arranged a meeting with him?"

"If you are free, we have a tentative date for next Wednesday morning."

"Sure, that's good. Now what is this cryptic 'S.N. → Fair…' you have added to the bottom of our agenda?" asked Portia.

Tureen smiled.

"Oh, that stands for Sneath Naydir to get Fairoin®."

"So?"

"He is scheduled to meet my contact tonight to acquire that controlled substance."

"Oh, right! That little scheme you concocted to turn the table on him." Portia always enjoyed that expression. She envisioned a colonial innkeeper actual turning over the dining table and converting it into a bed with a straw mattress.

"Yes," Tureen added. "If it goes as planned, Sneath will be on his way to the back alleys of Georgetown late this evening."

Susanne Naydir remained angry about the toe-sucking incident. She refused to speak with him at all for a day and a half thereafter, allowing Sneath to search his fevered brain for a plausible reason for attacking her tasty hallux. It seemed clear to him that it would be imprudent to admit to this harmless quirk, given his wife's reaction when she awoke. Better to provide a reasonable excuse. By the evening of the second post-incident day, he approached Susanne with a story that he believed had the ring of truth.

"Sweetie," he said, "I am so embarrassed about that crazy thing I did the other night. I guess I have to chalk it up to being pretty drunk and under the influence of a program I watched on the extreme sports channel at the bar."

Stony silence, but she at least had not turned away.

"It was this news flash about a guy who was selling unlaundered stockings worn by players in the 'TOP Girls' lacrosse league—you know, the one where they all wear teeny bikini tops. Apparently, there are people who have fetishes about girls' soiled intimate garments, but all bras and panties were sold out."

Susanne's eyes widened as though she had discovered a beetle in her quiche. However disgusting it might be, she was aware of the trade in soiled women's undergarments. What began in Tokyo as the sale of such items in tasteful plastic containers from vending machines blossomed on the ultranet (the secure VHS—very high speed—third gen exclusive and costly entry point to the galactic web) into a fashionable collectible for well-heeled perverts. Susanne had noticed a headline about the shocking parties such perverts enjoyed on a three-dimensional display next to the checkout lane at the market. Fleeting images of corpulent men sniffing unmentionables from crystal goblets caught her eye. Fortunately for Sneath, Susanne was aware of the entrepreneurial commerce he described. Instead of rolling her eyes in disbelief, she nodded slightly. He had permission to continue.

"Well, I was feeling no pain, looking down on the lights of the city, when the Selfer® brought me home. For no particular reason, I began wondering what could be so special about the smell of women's feet that made people pay good money for soiled athletic socks. You've got to admit, it is an intriguing question."

Susanne's wrinkled nose and glowering look confirmed that she was unprepared to admit it was an intriguing question.

"It is disgusting and perverted—that's what it is," she advised.

"Just so. Just so," agreed Sneath. "On the other hand, I understand that respectable people actually enjoy the olfactory experience. There's something exciting about it, and it's harmless."

Sneath realized he was beginning to lose Susanne's attention. Hurriedly, he added, "But, there I was, the other night, tipsy and seeing you looking so serene, sleeping on the couch with your bare toes exposed. I was overwhelmed with a need to check those toes out for myself—to understand the attraction they held for other men."

Susanne tilted her head to one side as her eyes narrowed. Sneath suspected her internal bullshit meter was approaching the red zone, but he plowed on.

"So, God forgive me, I licked your pinky. It was as soft as your earlobe and smelled like Edam cheese. The next thing I knew, I moved to your big toe and was compelled to put my lips around it like a little breast. I could feel the ridges of your toe print, and the smell of Edam filled my nostrils. Your toenail was so smooth, so different from your flesh, my tongue moved back and forth…"

Sneath had lost control. His planned story of an innocent experiment intended to mollify his irritated wife grew wings of its own. His excuse sailed into the realm of his true sensations. His eyes developed a soft sheen and his breath quickened.

Susanne saw that he had entered an almost trance-like state while rhapsodizing about her toes, and it frightened her. What else did she not know about the man who had fathered her children? As Sneath recovered himself, she backed away, wary about providing him further access to her feet, resolved to address her fob to learn more about toe sucking.

Sneath weakly concluded his story.

"So that's all it was. A stupid little experiment by your drunk husband. Won't happen again. We can just put this behind us, right?"

Susanne refused to answer.

Elever Snoddy had been Frank Crouch's invaluable scientific adviser for almost two decades. Over those years, he had recommended investments in many areas of scientific research that promised important commercial applications. Highly successful were the Terratron satellite that digitally peeled away the earth's layers to disclose the riches beneath, and molecule-sized robots that repaired many internal human organs. Their global positioning software automated vehicular travel and provided Selfers® with their enviable low fatality rates. Brainwave actuators challenged pharmaceuticals in reducing depression and enhancing pre-partum intelligence. Suspended-animation prison cells dramatically lowered the costs of incarceration. These successful investments proposed by Snoddy enhanced his reputation in the company and made him one of Frank Crouch's most trusted advisors.

He kept Frank informed about the latest advances in the fields of energy production, mineral extraction, and many other areas of interest to the Crouch

Empire. He was also helpful in arranging persuasive scientific studies that challenged the findings of government regulatory agencies that monitored Crouch businesses. Snoddy reported directly to Frank; Fred and Fergus were either intimidated by or uninterested in what he had to report.

Today, Snoddy focused on the energy areas of the company businesses. Frank could tell the news was not good. Snoddy, never cheerful, pressed the corners of his mouth almost to his jawbone, creating fat wrinkles that emphasized his woeful expression.

Frank turned toward the scientist as he sat and arranged virtual folders on the conference table.

"You look like you just swallowed dog shit, Lev. What's going on?"

"Frank, you recall that we decided a few years ago that hydrocarbons as sources of energy ultimately would be replaced by other, more efficient sources. Not solar, wind, water, biomass, or that sort of stuff, but some kind of nuclear reaction. Such sources would, by definition, be more efficient and less dangerous than the nuclear reactors we used before the one in California slid into the Pacific when the San Andreas Fault let go."

"Sure," said Frank, "that's when we invested in that startup in Alabama that was developing the advanced molten salt reactor, the process that uses zirconium or something."

"Zirconium hydride," noted Snoddy. "That is exactly what I wish to review today. The good news is that they have successfully operated their commercial reactor for six months with excellent results. They can generate seventy-five times more electricity per ton of mined uranium than our outmoded reactors. Installation costs were high, but operating costs are miniscule. The time to amortize the investment is about four years, with a thirty percent-plus return on our investment after that—and our cost of electricity will be less than a tenth of current rates. Of course, consumer rates would be appropriately higher."

Frank smiled and nodded to Snoddy. "Looks like another feather in your cap, Lev. Better than we expected!"

Surprisingly, the scientist maintained his gloomy expression. He reached for another folder, thought better of it, and relied on his fob instead. Snoddy would probably never be comfortable working in a paper-free environment.

He glanced at his fob and retinized the data he needed.

"The thing is, Frank, that although the Alabama project represents an astounding breakthrough, a parallel scientific discovery with even better results has just been reported from an unexpected area. I have been advised, in great confidence, that a team of UN scientists in Latvia has perfected nuclear fusion using a Tokamak generator. It is not common knowledge, but using radio frequency heating, they have achieved the very high temperatures necessary to energize the superheated plasma in a donut-shaped sphere, controlling the plasma using a magnetic field. I know, the technology has been around for years, but they have successfully miniaturized the process. It now seems…"

Frank interrupted.

"Lev, you lost me at superheated plasma. Break this down for me. How does this affect our molten salt reactor?"

"In a nutshell, Frank, these UN scientists have created a fusion reactor about the size of a home furnace that generates an unlimited amount of electricity at almost no cost. The reactor fuel is in air, and, once the machine starts, the energy it creates feeds itself and creates abundant electricity. For consumers it would be like having a little sun in their basement that provides all the energy they will ever need."

Frank immediately understood how this discovery limited the usefulness of their reactor. Perhaps there was a silver lining.

"How much do you think one of those 'little suns' would cost a consumer?"

Snoddy quickly found the estimate.

"Well, the prototype cost about three billion, but the 1.1 model, in full production, would be in the range of the cost of a miniCopter[1] one finds in almost every garage. The thing is, since it is a UN project, the technology will be freely available to qualified manufacturers anywhere. If past is prologue, once those wily Afganians learn the technology, the price is sure to drop."

---

1 MiniCopter—the mature version of drones employed to deliver packages. An enlarged four-propeller airborne conveyance capable of carrying three hundred pounds, outfitted for a person or cargo. Luxury versions are "Selfers®."

One of the qualities that distinguished Frank Crouch from his competitors was his sense of perspective and refusal to dwell on failure or defeat. He spent more time analyzing business successes than conducting post mortems on mistakes. For executives responsible for such mistakes, however, punishment began with crucifixion and escalated from there.

Frank spent long moments considering the information Snoddy provided. He thanked the scientist for his report, dismissed him, and conferred with his brother, Fred, about tax write-offs for development costs.

The following morning Frank met with his most trusted assistants. His message was clear. Sell their interest in the molten salt reactor to that grandson of Rupert Murdoch who was so eager to enter the modern energy industry, and use whatever means necessary to obtain the technology and manufacturing know-how for the Tokamak generator. Crouch Industries were going into the "little sun" business.

And, as Frank reminded Fred and Fergus, these developments in the creation of inexpensive energy reinforced his prediction that water would be the oil and gas of the future.

"It is a finite resource," he said, "and the more we control the better it will be for our business. When this damn Parks Act finally passes, we are going to control every place where water can be stored: Grand Canyon, Yellowstone, Niagara Falls, and places in between."

That afternoon he spoke with Sneath Naydir and a select group of legislators who owed their livelihood to their benefactor, Crouch Industries. Frank made two suggestions that, under the circumstances, carried the force of law. First, cut through the arcane self-imposed procedural crap that encrusted congressional action like barnacles on the hull of a speedboat, and pass the Parks Act. Second, encourage the Parks Department to prepare for the inevitable auction of the parks to assure swift accomplishment of the sales. Of course, Frank would be kept in the loop.

Noble Ferrari appeared tired as his eyes met Agatha's. The sharp definition of her fob reception emphasized the lines around his mouth and shadows under his eyes.

"What may I do for you this morning, Noble?" she asked.

"Well, I just received a letter signed by forty-one senators demanding to know what steps we have taken to prepare for the immediate and effective disposition of surplus property as required by the Parks Act."

"How so? They haven't even passed the act. And even if they had, and it was approved by the president, there is a one-year grace period before sales can begin. And then, the act provides for the incremental disposition of the 'surplus property,' ten percent of the land area each year. I understand why you're bothered," said Agatha.

"There is that, of course, but it is also galling," he said, "to have them meddling in purely administrative affairs. Congressional power is limited to passing laws, spending money, and trying to impeach the occasional president. It is obvious they don't know jack shit about running things. If they did, the nation wouldn't be in such dire straits."

Ferrari paused, then added, "I suppose that is for attribution," in recognition of the strong possibility that his comments were being recorded.

"I also had a conversation with Senator Hatchett. She recalled that I was a holdover from the previous administration, asked me if I enjoyed being secretary, and reinforced the seriousness of the letter from the senators. That woman has a vocabulary that would make a sailor's parrot blush."

Agatha moved her finger across the receptor pad of her fob, and the fob replied with a cheerful burp.

"Noble, I have forwarded a copy of the purchase order for the services of CGI to prepare the national parks auction, when and if. It is a huge consulting company that has done substantial government work in the past. They orchestrated the rollout of the Affordable Care Act many years ago."

"You mean that notorious failure in management and design? *That* CGI?"

"I guess that's the one," she acknowledged with a casual shrug. "Somehow that slipped my mind until you mentioned it. They have done much government work."

So, realized Noble, Agatha had already found a way to sabotage the sale of the nation's patrimony. What an exceptional administrator she was!

"Thank you, Agatha. I will provide that information to the senators. They will be relieved to learn that the situation is well in hand."

A CLOSE CALL

Sneath was unsure about the dress code for purchasing controlled substances. He suspected that information would be freely available from his all-knowing fob, but did not wish to broadcast his intentions to anyone watching his exchanges. His wife was unavailable to discuss a sartorial issue; she had not spoken to him since the toe incident and his ineffective excuses. He glanced again at the unfamiliar Georgetown address for the meeting. Somewhere near the university, he thought. He couldn't go wrong with business casual wear; he would imitate the college lecturers who added a touch of tweed to their outfits, setting the tone for the hundreds of thousands of students who attended each colossal virtual fob-based course offered by the university.

Sneath chose slacks and a shirt in the latest design. Concocted of cellulose, chicken feathers, and recycled household waste, faux-cotton cloth was favored by exclusive clothiers as a substitute for the long staple pima cotton that was now unavailable—the victim of overaggressive genetic engineering. Sneath enjoyed the silky feel of his new Brooks Brothers clothes, and their slight musky odor was hardly noticeable. He pulled on a loose-fitting sleeveless jerkin with tweed epaulettes and secured his fob in its special pocket. He decided to wear his new gyro-roamers—stabilized athletic shoes constructed of synthetic bison hide. He programmed them to correct his tendency to walk duck-like, with his feet pointed outward, and set the autolift feature to medium high. It always took a few minutes to become accustomed to the springing sensation as the roamers effortlessly pushed him forward.

His fob confirmed that the necessary bitcoins were on deposit in his personal account. Sneath disliked virtual currency. Not only was it unregulated and as negotiable as bearer bonds but, when the coins left his control, there was no evidence he had ever transferred them. That, of course, was why his banking clients paid him to promote deregulation of bitcoins. An unregulated, untraceable, untaxable virtual currency was every banker's wet dream. Instant transfer of the coins from one fob to another made them an orgiastic paradise.

Susanne pretended not to notice that her husband was leaving their home. The temperature of her cold shoulder was in the range of liquid nitrogen, and Sneath instantly recognized that no thaw was in evidence.

"Just going to meet with a new client for dinner over in Georgetown. Shouldn't be more than an hour or two," he said.

Suzanne stopped programming the KitchenWiz® to create the evening meal for her family, glared at Sneath, and reduced the servings by one, pressing the pad so forcefully that her finger turned white.

"Thanks for the short notice, *connard*," she hissed.

Suzanne was too well bred to curse in English. However, she permitted herself to use vulgar French when the occasion demanded. It always provided welcome relief.

Her husband did not understand "*connard*" exactly, though the meaning was clear. As he closed the door behind him, he guessed at his status. It would be way past asshole, he thought. Somewhere in the mother sucker range. He sighed and walked to the Selfer® pickup platform two blocks from his home. The orange vehicle was there already, blinking its purple light in welcome.

Holster Fenwick was one of Tureen's unrequited lovers. He was a professor of romance philology at Jefferson University, but his recreational passion was acting in local theater. Because of his unfortunate overbite and sallow complexion, directors usually cast him as a villain. Holster did not mind being typecast; he was happy performing on the stage, in any role.

He met Tureen when her firm hired him to provide guidance in the selection of trade names for a woman's chemical depilatory to be marketed by one of their clients in Europe. They wanted to avoid troublesome linguistic issues suffered by other international manufacturers such as when Standard Oil introduced "Exxon" abroad. The new name was immediately associated with a double cross and its negative implications.

In the process, Holster worked with Tureen, who was chief lobbyist for Amalgamated Corrosives. They had two working lunches together, enough for Holster to develop a wild romantic passion for Tureen, which she recognized as business as usual. She was cordial and friendly and did nothing to encourage such feelings. However, it was her policy not to discourage them either. One never knew when it would be helpful to have an unrequited lover who was good at romance languages and loved acting.

So, as she formulated the plan of attack on Sneath Naydir, Holster came to mind. He loved the idea of playing a disreputable drug dealer in aid of Tureen's practical joke on her fellow lobbyist. He secretly hoped a time would come when Tureen and he would be intimate and could laugh together about his performance. In the meantime, Holster was delighted to meet with his redheaded inamorata to go over her plan and employ needed bit players. The setting for their little drama would be his townhouse in Georgetown.

Sneath confirmed that he had the correct address and climbed the seven stone steps to the front door of the townhouse on the leafy side street in Georgetown. The streetlights were just beginning to glow and he glanced furtively down the street, surprised at this middle-class neighborhood drug dealership. A buzzer rang inside and the door cracked open, revealing a man with ferret-like teeth and a sharp nose wearing a "wifebeater" undershirt and pajama pants. To provide a more sinister appearance, Holster applied a purple scar to his left cheek and wore a large gold earring. He was pleased to see Sneath recoil as he pulled the door open and leaned toward his visitor, exhaling unpleasant fumes from the garlic clove popped into his mouth moments before.

"You Sneath?" he growled.

Sneath confessed he was.

"Get your ass in here," he said, checking the street as though he was concerned that Sneath had been followed.

Sneath entered a darkened foyer.

"Fob goes on the table and then I check you for devices," said Holster, burrowing into his role, relishing the sensation of developing a new character.

Holster motioned for Sneath to spread his legs and stand with arms outstretched, palms upward. Gruffly he searched for "devices," sending a painful jab to his victim's nether regions.

"OK. You're clean. Show me you got the five hunnert," Holster demanded, creating what he thought was a Eurasian accent.

"Five hundred? You told me it would be four hundred," complained Sneath.

"You keep bitchin', mother, it gonna be six hunnert another min! Show me you got them bits or I kick your ass outahere."

Cowed, Sneath recovered his fob and projected the balance of bits in his account onto the dim wall of the foyer.

"Umm, looks like you got five hunnert sixty seven bits on you. That would cover it all right. Send them over. Here's the code," proclaimed Holster, channeling his account code to Sneath's fob. Sneath's account instantly rolled back to zero.

Holster disappeared through a door at the end of the foyer, leaving Sneath standing in the darkened room nursing his still throbbing crotch. He waited long enough to question whether this unpleasant man had simply disappeared with his money. Just as panic began to set in, Holster returned, holding a clear plastic bag containing a powdery ivory substance, which he held out to Sneath.

"Top drawer, number one synthesized Fairoin. So good it makes you cry for your mother," said Holster, deeply in character.

Sneath accepted the bag of baby laxative, searched for the exit, wishing desperately to leave this dim room, this repulsive drug dealer. Holster leaned past his visitor, offering a last whiff of garlic, permitting its burned rubberband aroma to encircle Sneath, and opened the door. The cool air of dusk revived him as he moved down the steps to the sidewalk, now bathed in artificial light.

He tucked the bag of ivory powder into the pocket of his jerkin and walked toward the subway station, which was much closer than the Selfer® stop.

A large man stepped out of the entranceway to a basement apartment and stood between Sneath and the subway entrance. He held up a wallet that flashed ominously in the yellow light of a street lamp. Sneath's heart sank and his bowels threatened to open.

"Excuse me, sir," said the large man, "would you mind if I ask you a few questions?"

"Yes" was what he wanted to say. "No, not at all" came out. Instinctively, Sneath glanced behind, a concession to a primitive fight-or-flee response. An even larger man had materialized a few paces away, blocking an escape along the sidewalk. Both men converged on Sneath, prodding him to a spot beneath a streetlight where Sneath inappropriately focused on moths and gnats thudding into the bright sodium vapor light above.

"Could I see some identification, please," said large man number one as large man number two stood aside, scowling ominously.

Sneath fumbled with the flap of an inner pocket on his jerkin, causing number one to move his hand beneath his too-tight jacket.

"Just take out your fob with two fingers, very slowly."

Completely flustered, Sneath let the fob slip though thumb and forefinger. It was saved from smashing on the pavement by the anti-gravity app he had installed two weeks earlier. The fob wobbled, suspended six inches above the cement, where number one retrieved it and expertly pressed the activator to examine Sneath's vital statistics.

"Can you tell me, Mr. Nadir, what business you have in this neighborhood?" he asked.

Sneath gulped, trying to lubricate the Sahara his mouth had become. His tongue seemed permanently welded to the roof of his mouth, and no words came. He tried clearing his throat.

Not receiving a response, number one added, "You see, we observed you visiting the address of a known drug dealer, 'Snake' Fenwick, and we need to know what you were doing there."

Number two intensified his scowl and spoke in a gravelly bass. "Yeah. Doing there."

Sneath faced insipient incontinence. It had not occurred to him that he might need a cover story to explain his presence in middle-class Georgetown. Tightening his anal sphincter and trying to fabricate a plausible story at the same time almost undid him. However, the crisis abated and he explained how he was meeting a colleague for dinner and had mistaken the location of his home. He stumbled upon "Snake" by accident and agreed that he was an unpleasant person. To emphasize that point he pointed down the street and shook his head. That was enough to dislodge the plastic bag with ivory powder from the pocket of his jerkin, and it fell to his feet, almost in the same place his fob had quivered moments before.

Number two pounced on the bag and waved it under Sneath's nose.

"This yours, asshole?" he asked. It was a rhetorical question.

Sneath steeled himself as number two clamped his hand around his upper arm.

"You're under arrest, and I am about to martinize you," he stated. Number two had not mastered his script thoroughly and confused a critical word.

Number one quickly added a correction. "Yeah, we're gonna Mirandize you under Miranda II." He linked his fob with Sneath's and transferred the Miranda warning that now included the right to contact a preferred assistor. He returned the fob to Sneath, demanding he read the warning and signify understanding by adding his thumbprint. Sneath raised a shaking hand and pressed his thumb against the fob. He had aged ten years since exiting the drug dealer's townhouse.

Number one adjusted his fob to facial recognition and linked it to his victim's personal data. A flash, and Sneath's DPI (Digital Photo Information) was embedded with his other data. As far as Sneath was concerned, he was indelibly marked as a felony two criminal.

As his captors trundled him toward a black van parked on the street, Sneath became overwhelmed with self-pity. His wife had discovered his secret fetish; his mistress was developing frequent headaches; his main employer, Frank Crouch, was expressing disappointment with his lobbying efforts; and now he was facing ultimate ignominy and a possible prison sentence. It was so unfair! Moisture dripped from his eyes and nose made his shirt and jerkin wet and gooey. His optimistic gyro-roamers infuriated him, pushing his feet upward and forward, helping his captors shove him toward the black van. He felt helpless, out of control, infantile. He wished his mommy were there, to make it all better. Sneath was weeping as his captors shoved him into the back of the van. One and two smiled at each other. This had gone really well!

Number one said, "Stay put, faggot. We're gonna take a leak before driving to the station. And we're taking this shit with us." Number two waved the plastic bag with the incriminating powder in Sneath's face and slammed the van door.

The two burly actors then walked away.

Sneath was alone in the backseat of what he believed was a locked van. He waited, tears rolling down his cheeks, heart racing, hands shaking, sinking into depths of misery. Though his brain was not firing on all cylinders, he grasped the part of the Miranda warning that he could call a preferred assistor. He considered calling Nestor Fairchild, his firm's legal counsel, for help. However, he paused before pressing the contact button on his fob. Nestor represented his firm, not him. It was possible he would feel obliged to advise the partners of Sneath's arrest as a drug felon. Partners had been ousted for much lesser offenses, mainly for stealing the firm's money.

Then he thought of Tureen. Of course! She was discreet and knew everyone. She was his conspirator. He wouldn't be sitting in the back of this van but for her. She would be his salvation. Hope arrived afresh as he found her channel.

The actors had just told Tureen about the outcome of Sneath's "arrest" when his unexpected call arrived.

Feigning surprise, she answered, "Hello, Sneath. How did everything go tonight? Are you back home now?"

Sneath announced that he definitely was *not* back home and related, at length, his current intolerable situation, emphasized by the occasional sigh and blubber.

All compassion and concern, Tureen said, "Give me a couple minutes. Sit tight. I'll get back to you as soon as possible."

Sneath, relieved, prepared to wait. He was beginning to wonder when his captors would drive him to the police station.

Tureen opened a bottle of Borolo, poured a glass, and took a few sips before calling Sneath back.

"Listen. Don't look around. Get over to the passenger side and open the door. Yes. It's fixed. Get out and go home. This never happened. I cashed in a few chips. I understand, and you are welcome. Go home. Get a good night's sleep."

The Borolo tasted especially delicious that night.

INSIDE THE BELTWAY

Melvin Salmon nervously awaited his reunion with Portia Merson. Though he had followed her activities in detail for many years, he had not actually seen her or a good image of her since she defended him against hacking charges. He was afraid that romantic fantasies colored his recollection of her, that the current Portia would not meet his glorified expectations. He knew she was married, but what if she had grown fat or developed facial hair? Maybe warts? What if she did not even remember him?

The door to the conference room opened and a striking redheaded woman strode in. Not Portia. She must be the one who contacted him, Tureen something. He stood and accepted her offered hand, glancing away for a moment to check the open door for someone else, for Portia. She was not there.

Tureen motioned him to a chair and said, "Thank you so much for visiting with us. As I mentioned during our talk, Portia and I would very much like to discuss your interest in the Parks Act, and especially your relationship with Senator Hinckle."

Her comment startled Melvin. His eyes widened and his head came up as he looked at the smiling Tureen.

"Senator Hinckle?" he asked. "What makes you think…"

"Come on, Melvin. You know there are no secrets inside the beltway that last longer than the time it takes to push a fob contact button. As far as we are concerned, you did a good thing in helping the senator come to the right decision. Portia and I just want to be sure that we are contacting all possible allies as part of our mandate to stop the Parks Act. You look like one of the good guys and we hope to work with you."

He lost his concern about Tureen's knowledge of his connection with Senator Hinckle at the prospect of "working with" Portia.

As though on cue, Portia concluded a conversation with an assistant and moved through the door to the conference room, projecting friendliness, energy, and a slightly bulging belly poorly concealed by the retro scarlet A-frame dress she wore. Melvin gulped. She was more beautiful than he remembered, more enchanting, more...

"Oh, Melvin, how good it is to see you looking so well," Portia cooed. "I have read all about your many successes. I am very proud of you."

She came close and offered a welcoming hug. Melvin responded and patted her back, then pulled quickly away and sat, worried about a growing tumescence and the sudden weakness in his knees. The various introductory remarks he had rehearsed raced through his mind. The preparatory pep talk he had given himself before entering the office rang in his ears. He cleared his throat.

"Urp," he said. "I mean, uh, urp."

Portia took her seat and Tureen offered him a bottle of cold water, which he swallowed hastily until his voice returned.

"Sorry. Must not be used to the air-conditioning. What I want to say is that I am so happy to see you again, too, Ms. Merson..."

"Portia, please!" she interrupted.

"Portia." The name felt like distilled honey on his tongue. "Portia, I am forever grateful for your help in escaping that hacking charge in college. When I come across information about you and your projects from time to time, I read it carefully. I know from your op-ed piece in the *Post* that you strongly oppose the Parks Act."

Portia leaned toward him across the table, showing her eagerness to hear his every word. Encouraged, Melvin began to spin out his story of the Hinckle encounter.

"So, I had this opportunity to meet with the senator on a related matter a while ago and our conversation turned to the Parks Act. I'm happy to say that I provided him with new information that helped him change his position and oppose the act. Knowing how you felt about the act, I thought you would appreciate hearing about his change of heart. Hinckle agreed to let your office know."

Reconsidering that action, Melvin now realized it had not been very astute. If Tureen knew about his involvement, others probably did also. Seeing Portia sitting across from him, he became aware that he had involved her as well. Shit, he thought, no good deed goes unpunished in this town.

"It seemed like the right thing to do then—not so much now," he admitted, "since others know you were involved."

"Of course, not a problem—and thank you for helping as you did. Hinckle's defection from the 4-H Club was a great help to our position. We sincerely appreciate it," said Portia.

Tureen nodded assent, and both women smiled thanks for Melvin's public-spirited support.

Neither believed that a simple conversation with Senator Hinckle had influenced him to alter his vote on the act. They began a subtle cross-examination, probing his relationship with the senator, trolling for tidbits of information to create a mosaic of Melvin, cajoling snippets of personal revelation. To help Tureen's examination, Portia interjected an occasional encouraging word— "amazing," "bold," "clever," even "brilliant." After about twenty minutes of ego elevation, Melvin was primed, by the high regard in which these women held him, to reveal further acts of individual heroism.

"Well, one of the first government jobs I had after AEROTICA became successful was back in '14 when I took a contract with the CIA. That was when the Senate was wrapping up its analysis of the CIA's torture program. You know, using secret documents and interviews with people involved in the torture business. So, the guys at CIA sort of lost track of all the stuff the senators had collected and wanted a heads-up about what the Senate report might say. It was, like, to prepare a rebuttal, not be blindsided, that sort of thing."

Melvin warmed inwardly as he recalled this rewarding government contract.

"I got called in to show them how to access information in the computers used by the senators and their aides. Preview conclusions and whatnot."

"You mean you hacked the Senate computers!" Portia exclaimed. "Melvin, you're incorrigible." But she smiled as she said it.

"Yes, but that's all that I did. I didn't delete a lot of stuff the CIA guys wanted to disappear. I am an ethical person, after all."

Tureen said, "But that report, as I recall, concluded that torture was ineffective and illegal, and that the CIA outright lied to the White House, Congress, and the American people."

"You're right," said Melvin, "but the CIA sent a well-prepared response the minute the report came out to all reporters. The press had to report both sides. That diluted the full effect of the Senate report, and not a single CIA head rolled."

Melvin offered a satisfied smile. "I got a bonus and a secret citation. Contained the damage, I did."

Portia and Tureen, fascinated by Melvin's story but wary of his moral compass, pressed for more details of his work with the government.

"Let's see," he said. "Remember how there were almost no issues with whistle-blowers during the Obama administration? Yours truly designed an app for all administration communication devices from laptops to smart phones that identified, recorded, and transmitted possible unauthorized communications. Suspected messages went to a basement office in the West Wing."

Tureen, never a supporter of the Obama presidency, interrupted.

"This was done without the government employee's knowledge?"

"Oh, they knew all right," said Melvin. "All the devices belonged to the government, to us taxpayers, and the users signed a seven-page confidentiality agreement that included a 'no whistle-blowing' clause. I made sure it was all perfectly legal."

"So," said Portia, "for example, anyone calling a reporter would be suspected of whistle-blowing?"

"Right. I gotta tell you, it was a very successful project. Many people left their jobs early, including two cabinet secretaries."

Melvin chuckled at his recollection.

"After a while people figured out there was something odd about their government-issue communicators, and they reverted to face-to-face meetings for sensitive issues. Of course, standard surveillance devices in restaurants, streets, and such captured most of that. Come to think of it, maybe that's how you learned about my meeting with Senator Hinckle. Like you said—no secrets inside the beltway."

Portia and Tureen exchanged a glance that confirmed appreciation of their guest's formidable and dangerous talents. They were about to press on when Melvin asked to excuse himself to release the cups of coffee he had rented during their conversation. An assistant escorted him from the room.

"Your friend is some piece of work," offered Tureen. "Do you believe his stories?"

"Don't be so jaded," said Portia. "I know it's easy to be cynical when we deal with politicians all the time. Their stories almost never have the added benefit of being true. Melvin, though, is being mostly honest, I think. Of course, the bit about persuading Senator Hinckle is hogwash. There is a lot more there…"

Melvin returned, eager to bask further in the two women's hero worship. As he sat, he moved his chair closer to Portia.

"I've been thinking of other government stuff I've done and how it might be helpful here," he said. "Remember last year when two senators got electric shocks when they put their voting cards into the slots at their desks?"

Portia recalled that what the Senate first thought to be a terrorist plot turned out to be the result of faulty wiring by the lowest-bidding contractor.

"Well, you know that legislators use their ID cards with chips to vote at their desks or at personal terminals in their home districts. It is supposed to be as secure and foolproof as making payments with a fob. Last year, a family of Norway rats living in the basement of the Senate chamber penetrated the main computer of that outdated system and shorted out a handful of terminals. When the senators inserted their cards, a new high-voltage circuit was completed. Fried their cards and cost the junior senator from Puerto Rico a pinky finger. There's nothing like losing a finger to get the Senate's attention."

Fascinated with these revelations, the two women encouraged Melvin to continue.

"It seems that a number of senators knew about the intricate encoding involved in the AEROTICA program, and their security detail contracted us to update and enhance the legislature's internal voting system. Just a few months ago, we completed a complex and redundant system of remote computers with the capacity for quadrillions of FLOPS to monitor and control all those terminals. In addition to foolproof voting capabilities, we added features like emoticons, requests for favors from the candy desk, information about the availability of stalls in the cloakroom, the physical location of missing senators...that sort of thing. Enhanced functionality and a homey touch. And, of course, totally secure and hacker-proof. It is clearly the best thing my company has done."

Melvin paused, expecting applause and approbation. Portia and Tureen, however, seemed befuddled, unsure why Melvin felt this information was important. First disappointed, then understanding, Melvin added a crucial bit of information.

"Oh, you probably don't know about the back door. With a system as complex and sophisticated as this, we programmers always include a back door—a way to access the code and repair any glitches or errors that might arise. It also lets us update the system as improvements occur."

Clarity brightened the women's outlook.

"So, what you are saying is that you can control the Senate's voting program. Like, override the actual vote?" asked Portia.

"Yes. You got that right."

Benjamin Franklin Chang stared moodily across Hong Kong Harbor, watching lights from tall buildings surrounding dark waters challenge encroaching dusk. He had dimmed the lights in his penthouse office to observe the approach of nightfall without glaring reflections. Most evenings he thought happily on the day's events, mainly by assessing how his numerous ventures were prospering. Prostitution, drugs, and gambling were growth industries, adding constantly to his bottom line. Tonight, however, was not a time to be joyful. The popularly elected leadership of the one and a half billion residents of the People's Democracy of China had initiated another moral values crackdown and recently shuttered all his operations in the lands to the north, causing the loss of millions of renminbi.

Since he had to relocate thousands of employees, he now urgently needed to acquire properties in the United States. It was more urgent than acquiring U.S. citizenship and getting reimbursed for his lost yacht. Although he could find temporary employment for his people in less desirable venues like Canada, the Netherlands, Australia, and Brazil, the real money was in America.

He reminded Tureen O'Porto of his vital need to acquire suitable parks property a few days earlier. In his current state of distress he was not mollified by her many reasons why he needed to be patient. She seemed insincere—not the confident and dominant woman he lusted for.

"Is there something you are not telling me?" he asked. "Tell me now. I can help fix it. You know I have assets there."

"Come on, Ben. Even you can't intimidate the American Congress. Let me do my job. Everything will be all right."

"Do your damn job then. But do it quickly. My patience is running thin," he said darkly.

He stared at Tureen's breasts as she faded from view.

Now, in his dimmed office, he flicked a button on his desk and watched a hologram of Sylvester Chu materialize in front of his desk. His Washington lawyer, balding and slightly stooped, made a little bow, offered good wishes, and commiserated about the unfortunate action of the Chinese leaders.

"Right. Enough of this. Did you make the inquiries I asked?" Chang said impatiently.

"I did."

Rotten lawyers, thought Chang. Only answer the question asked. Never volunteer anything. Son of a bitch!

"So, what did you learn?" he asked heatedly.

"It appears your friend may be suffering from mixed allegiances when it comes to the Parks Act. For example, she represents a faction of western state governors who pay her to lobby against the Parks Act. And she was in the front ranks of the march against the Parks Act."

"AGAINST!" roared Chang.

"So it appears."

"APPEARS?"

"Yes. There is additional evidence that your lobbyist is associating herself with a Portia Merson, a bleeding-heart liberal with an undistinguished law degree who works to defeat the Parks Act. Additionally, we can find no evidence of any pending legislation to secure citizenship for you. In sum, we are confident that Ms. O'Porto is not necessarily acting in your best interests."

"So, that's definitive," mocked Chang.

"Insofar as it goes, I would agree," offered Chu.

"You will let me know if anything develops, Parks Act-wise?"

"Of course. If there is nothing further at this point in time, I will take my leave."

Chang watched bitterly as the circumspect Chu's image dissolved. Lights of ferryboats showed in the harbor below, important little travelers coursing dark waters.

You have fucked with the wrong Chinaman, thought Chang, recreating Tureen's image from their last conversation on his fob. He pressed his thumb on her face so hard that the fob hardened to safe mode. "Enjoy that smile while you still have it, bitch," he muttered.

The boats scudded across the harbor on their cheery paths, scattering bioluminescent sea creatures.

Wylie looked from the amber liquid in his glass toward Senator Pete Rowe, at eighty-nine the oldest senator in Washington. He is showing his age, thought Wylie, watching as his friend shifted his body in an overstuffed leather chair, aging joints aflame. The skin beneath his jaw was loose and florid. It signaled the coming of fresh words with a subtle flutter. Now, both men enjoyed a companionable silence, Wylie sipping his scotch and the senator scowling at the cup of tea that long ago replaced his afternoon bourbon.

Rowe's jowls wobbled.

"Remind me, Wylie—what was it you were doing in California?"

"I was giving a talk about xeriscaping to the city planners for NewLA. You know, incorporating oleander, sage, ocotillo cactus, and bougainvillea in their planning. They…"

"Dammit, Wylie, talk American. You know better than to use those Greekified words with me. Speak plain!" demanded Rowe.

Wylie smiled. "Sorry, Pete, I apologize for slipping into pedantic mode. I was giving advice about drought-tolerant plants to the city planners there. Part of the outreach of one of my charities. They are trying hard to get the new city plan right. Even though it's been a eight years since the San Andreas Fault split and sent the old Los Angeles into the sea, the people are still shell-shocked. Rebuilding is slow and very emotional."

The senator nodded. "Unlucky bastards. Lose a good part of the state to the sea and still in the worst drought of the century. At least the desalination plants will be close to the new city."

Wylie looked sour. "Yes, but the extra salty water they return to the sea appears to be poisoning the bottom-feeders of the ocean. And all the money we put into renewable energy to run the plants was probably wasted, what with those commercial Tokamak things coming online next year."

"No free lunch, is there?" responded Rowe. "The only light at the end of that tunnel is the new taxes we are assessing for the cheap electricity produced by the reactors."

In fact, the Government Accountability Office predicted that all the revenue lost from greatly diminished taxes on carbon-based energy would be replaced threefold by the "T-mak" taxes. Some economists suggested that they offered a path to national solvency. All those in Congress who wanted to approve the Parks Act rejected those suggestions. They argued that they weren't economists and could therefore believe what "common sense" told them.

The senator was not finished quizzing Wylie about his trip.

"Tell me, is it true you can see some of the office towers of old LA in the ocean? Must be a hell of a sight."

It was a question asked of Wylie often when he returned from the new California shoreline.

"Yes, but not from NewLA. The office towers are now over sixty miles away in the ocean and you can only see about twelve or thirteen miles from the dunes. You can get a ferry to the area, though, and explore the city by mini-sub or scuba. I am too old for that stuff, but people say it is fascinating. Of course, federal agents are everywhere to keep looters at bay. They estimate there are billions of dollars' worth of jewelry on the corpses alone."

Both men contemplated that grim statistic. There were wildly diverse estimates of the number of lives lost in the earthquake. Millions, however, had surely died.

Rowe stared morosely through his office window at the sunlit Capitol beyond, and then turned toward his friend.

"There's some fresh activity on the Parks Act that hasn't been disclosed in the blogs yet. Things going on. Be a vote soon. You could tell Portia."

"That's not surprising. The vote has been delayed for almost six months already," noted Wylie.

"Well," added the senator, "that pissant junior senator from Puerto Rico... whatshisname...Julio Murphy, who lost his pinky finger, has been threatening to filibuster unless the sales are accelerated and a special exception is made for El Morro, El Yunque, and Cerro Gordo in his home state. The thing is, Deb Hatchett was fed up with all the delays, probably needed to assure continued funding by Crouch Industries, and set young Julio straight."

"Straight?" asked Wylie.

"She asked the pissant whether he wanted Frank Crouch in his corner or his opponent's come next election. He got the point quick as a frog on a June bug. The Senate will take up the Parks Act in about three weeks—as soon as they vote continuing appropriations for Syrian and Iranian reconstruction. The bookmakers are giving three to one odds the Parks Act will be approved."

"That is discouraging. I'll pass it on to Portia. She has worked her heart out on this issue. A loss will be very hard to take," said Wylie.

"There is one other tidbit," added Rowe. "Investigative reporters for the Times Blog have discovered that Deb Hatchett cooked the books at her apartment complexes to obtain over five million new dollars from HUD for affordable housing credits that were applied to luxury penthouses. Pretty strong evidence, too. She may be going down. Small loss, I say."

The two old men paused to examine their drinks. So, nothing new in Washington politics.

GRAND CANYON

Looking west from the outer rim of the Grand Canyon Skywalk, Portia and Grover saw thunderclouds rolling toward them above the Colorado River. From their vantage point four thousand feet above the canyon floor they saw clear sky above, cement gray clouds boiling like an unwatched pot, and torrents of rain pelting hikers far below.

"I've never seen that before," said Grover. "Sunny skies and lightning forking down from eye-level clouds. Awesome!"

Portia, already slightly queasy from peering almost a mile down through the glass beneath her feet, watched the approaching storm nervously. She cradled her swollen belly defensively with both hands.

"Grover, that thing is heading right toward us. Let's get under cover."

"Right," said Grover. He took Portia's arm to help her navigate the curved cantilevered bridge back to the rim of the canyon, to the large waiting room where they could watch the storm safely.

"Easy, boy!" she said. "Your future heir has me off balance. I'm waddling like a duck trying to balance a pumpkin. And being out here literally at the point of nowhere doesn't give me great confidence."

Grover guided her carefully to solid land and cover. The storm arrived quickly, lashing the large windows, pelting visitors who chose to remain on the bridge with gravely hail. Wind and rain swept away little piles of ice that collected on the bridge and sent them plummeting toward the canyon floor. Far below, in the green water of the river, Portia thought she could make out bright orange inflated boats bobbing on white caps.

"That couldn't be Tureen yet, could it?" she asked Grover, pointing down to the river.

"Not likely. She went in this morning much farther upriver. She probably won't be down there until day after tomorrow. I'm sure she's getting wet now, though, either from the rain or the river."

"She's welcome to it," said Portia. "There's no way you could get me on one of those rubber boats now. With my luck I'd have a water baby on the river."

Grover smiled at the thought. Water baby indeed! Although Portia's pediatrician assured them that the suborbital flight to Las Vegas was risk free, Grover still worried. Worried about the flight, about the seven thousand-foot altitude of the canyon rim, about Portia's ungainly walk on gravel paths, about their decision to join Tureen on this "lark" in a national park away from DC when the vote on the Parks Act was only three weeks away.

Portia, sitting on the bench, winced. "You OK?" he asked.

"Sure. I think your son needs a pedicure. It just felt as though he stabbed a kidney with a toenail. Here, feel here."

Grover placed his hand on her belly, ignoring the other people in the waiting room, and felt what? A knee, foot, elbow pushing against his palm.

"A lusty one," he announced proudly.

"Easy for you to say. You don't having a zygote using your large intestines as a playground."

Seeing Grover's worried look, she laughed and put her hand on his cheek. "Sorry for the hyperbole. Everything's OK. Just getting a little apprehensive about mister lusty and his approaching debut. Joking helps, I think."

"Sure." Grover was soothed, but concerned. "Shall we head back to the El Tovar Hotel?"

A shabby green school bus creaked to a stop outside the Skywalk and exchanged those arriving for those leaving. The bus carried them to the nearby heliport, where a military-style transporter lifted them above the south rim of the canyon to Grand Canyon Village. The recently approved flight path avoided the four-hour bus trip between the two locations.

Portia, at a window seat, saw that the storm had cleared, revealing the multihued walls of the mile-deep canyon in glowing afternoon sunlight.

"How beautiful!" she exclaimed. "How could anyone seriously agree to sell this off to the highest bidder? It makes me sick to think of what may happen in a few weeks."

"You and I have done everything possible to influence the outcome of the proposed legislation. It's maddening, but I can't think of anything more we can do. Maybe pray?" said Grover over the racket of the engines.

Portia compressed her lips as she considered a forbidding path, a possibility that ignored her legal training. There, on a helicopter cruising above one of nature's most awesome vistas, her baby poking a tender spot below her navel, holding back tears at the thought of losing such great beauty, Portia examined a classical ethical dilemma.

Suppose I managed to thwart the Parks Act illegally, she thought, with little or no chance of being caught. Would I be judged for the consequences of my actions or the actions themselves? I was taught that the ends do not justify the means, but surely there must be an exception. But no exception came to mind.

Tears welled in her eyes, submerging the astonishing view of rainbow-striated canyon walls in a watery film. Grover noticed immediately and was puzzled, concerned. He leaned across the tight seat of the helicopter to hug her shoulders.

Portia sniffled and said, "It's OK. Must be hormones or something."

She blinked, rubbed away the tears, and offered a little laugh.

"It's I don't know what…I am just overwhelmed by all this," she said, gesturing toward the horizon.

The helicopter landed, and Grover and Portia made their way through swirling red dust to the hotel van, both looking forward to rest and dinner. Portia held Grover's hand as they sat side by side in the van. A new thought had arrived. Should she discuss her ethical dilemma with her husband?

Her contact in the Arizona governor's office persuaded Tureen not to miss a three-day rafting trip on the Colorado River through the canyon.

"Awesome experience," she said. "The canyon is spectacular from water level, and running the rapids is thrilling. The hydraulics are pretty mild—only three or four number fives in the lower canyon. You're going to love it!"

In her enthusiasm to extol the glories of rafting, the contact failed to note that she had never gone—couldn't even swim. She lived vicariously through the stories she passed on. Eventually the stories became a parallel reality to a point where she became a participant. Been river rafting? Sure, she would say; it was awesome. Gotta go again soon. Wishful thinking made it so.

Charles Dodgson had it right. "What I tell you three times is true."[2]

Tureen was excited about the challenge of braving the river rapids. She purchased Quickdri™ shorts and shirts, a wide-brim hat that floated, rowing gloves, and a plastic device that allowed her to pee while standing up. She worked out on a StairMaster for almost two weeks and guzzled the latest version of muscle milk. She felt invigorated and ready as she boarded the space liner for Las Vegas with Portia and Grover.

After transferring from Las Vegas, they parted at the transport hub on the south rim of the canyon.

"I'll be back at El Tovar Tuesday about noon," Tureen told Portia. "I can take the funicular up from the bottom of the canyon, clean up, and meet you for lunch."

The pair wished her a safe adventure, and Tureen grabbed her new backpack for the hop across the canyon to the north rim, and then the descent from there to the Colorado River. She glanced again at the flyer provided by her contact in the governor's office.

Your Grand Canyon rafting vacation begins in the lower one hundred miles of the canyon. The famous rapids of the Colorado River are tamer here, and the scenery is especially beautiful. Massive sandstone cliffs are overhead and hidden waterfalls rush into the river. You can see blue herons, hawks, eagles, and bighorn sheep. At night, the Milky Way glows like a bright lantern in the firmament…

---

2 "The Hunting of the Snark" by Charles Lutwidge Dodgson, author of *Alice in Wonderland*

The shuttle landed near the entrance to the lodge at the north rim, and Tureen and a few other rafters carried their gear the short distance to the Bright Angel Trail head, where mechanical pack mules waited. A guide helped load the ungainly robots designed to navigate the tortuous switchback trail leading to the river. The rafters climbed into the six-wheelers that would carry them down, cautioned to avoid the flexible pleats that allowed the vehicles to move like caterpillars along the curved path. Halfway down the side on the canyon Tureen saw three lemon yellow inflatable rafts pulled up on a sandy bank. One would be her transportation for the next three days.

Three sturdy guides, two men and a woman, waited by the rafts for their passengers. The pack mule carrying Tureen's gear arrived and stopped near one of the rafts, and its guide carefully unloaded the metal animal and placed the gear on a tarp spread near the front of the raft.

"The eight lucky people who belong to this gear will have the pleasure of my company for the next three days as we raft along my river. Collect your stuff and us guides will begin your safety orientation and show you how to stay on the boats when we hit rapids. I hope you all are ready for the adventure of a lifetime! They call me 'Lance.'"

Lance Peppercorn had curly golden hair, twinkling hazel eyes, a smooth but stubbled tanned face, a firm bronzed body, and a large penis slightly bent downward two inches from the tip, all of which he used to good advantage. He was an American nomad, wandering from place to place and job to job, always searching for a new adventure. "Footloose and fancy free," he said. "No car, no house, no wife to slow me down."

But he was beginning to slow down, a little. Now in his early forties, Lance had moments when he realized his body would someday no longer satisfy the needs of a river rafter, wrangler, muleskinner, tracker, downhill racer, or whatever seasonal employment the great outdoors offered. Any day now, he thought, I'm gonna hafta think about the future.

Lance inventoried the eight fresh passengers for his inflatable boat. A young couple, honeymooners, no doubt. A man in his fifties with a girl in her twenties. Trophy something or other, he figured. He would know by trip's end. An older, fit, leathery couple. Had the right gear, well used. Experienced outdoor people;

no trouble there. A woman in early middle age carrying the latest moviemaking gear in an expensive waterproof bag. Probably the first one to go over when they hit a hydraulic. Have to watch out for her. A stunning redheaded woman in her mid-thirties. All-new outfit, proper gear, well-filled blouse. Not self-conscious or condescending; seemed like regular people. Very interesting.

Lance and the two other guides gathered the groups together and reminded them that they were here at Whitmore Wash and that their journey would end at Pearce Ferry, ninety-seven miles away. Then the guides explained the use of life jackets, helmets, and paddles, and showed the new rafters how to gain stability by wedging a foot into the crevice between the raft's floor and side.

Tureen practiced dipping her paddle into imaginary water, and then looked across the flowing green river to the steep multihued walls of the great chasm. I am a cliché, she thought, a small person in a huge wilderness, overwhelmed by the raw splendor of these surroundings. She felt a pleasing thrill of excitement move across her shoulders and down her spine. Is this, she wondered, what those tree huggers mean when they talk about getting high on nature?

Lance positioned his rafting group along the sides of the boat, placing Tureen in the left front, and shoved off into a calm eddy downstream from a bend. He commanded his crew to paddle in unison as he steered the boat with his oar.

"OK, you guys, we practice in calm water, but when we get into the flow of the river I can usually manage to keep us on an even keel," he said. "Remember that when we really get moving, I need to count on you to paddle on one side or the other. When we hit rapids, I'll deal. You concentrate on staying in the boat, feet wedged and holding onto the rope. If a hydraulic spits you out of the boat, stay on your back and one of us will get you."

The crew practiced in the calm water for another quarter hour, and then Lance guided the boat back to shore. The guides expertly stowed provisions for three days in the center of each boat. The travelers discovered that a "pit stop" meant relieving themselves at actual pits, using a trowel to bury their waste. The man with the young woman companion joked that the brochure failed to mention that detail. The young woman glared at her companion, which

Lance noted. Looks like the bluebird of paradise may become a cooked goose, he thought, gleefully mixing his metaphors.

Now hardened by a half hour of paddling practice, the crews of the three boats moved onto the river, feeling the bottom of the boats shudder as the current corrugated the pliable material beneath their feet.

"Oh," exclaimed Tureen as she pushed against the rushing water. "A foot massage from a wild river!" Happily, she thrust her paddle into the water, creating an unexpected splash that hit the person behind her, Mr. Manly, the seasoned adventurer. He splashed back. The newlyweds joined in and soon the boat was awash, its occupants thoroughly drenched and laughing.

"All right, children," said Lance. "It usually takes longer to get to the first water fight, but play time is now over. Our first rapid is just ahead, to the right of that bend. It's a number four with the added benefit of boulders, so stay sharp and hold on."

To Tureen the water ahead looked like a rippled infinity pool, blending with the far reaches of the canyon. Then, as the boat rounded a bend, she heard a loud rushing noise and saw the sharp drop of the river into a chute of boiling white water, cascading around gleaming boulders and creating a cauldron of back-rushing water at the bottom of the flow. She caught her breath, as though about to begin the first long drop on a roller coaster.

Lance expertly guided the boat through the center of the chute, its stubby nose pointed straight toward the churning water at the end of the run.

"Hold tight," he roared. "That's the hydraulic and it's going to swallow our nose and pop it up. Get a good grip, you people in front."

Tureen stowed her paddle, sat on her foot as the other was wedged into the boat, and held the rope along the side with both hands. As promised, the bulbous nose in front of her buried itself in the churning water, driven downward by the sheer force of the river's flow. Water cascaded into the boat over the bow, and the back of the boat moved skyward, lifting Lance six feet above the surface of the river. Suddenly, as though propelled by a mysterious force, the bow snapped upward like a pebble from a slingshot. Tureen emulated that pebble, lost her grip on the rope, felt her foot slip away from the boat, and flew helplessly over the green water before splashing into the river amid an explosion of bubbles.

Dazed and submerged, she saw the bright green water surrounding her and lazy eddies of bubbles playing along the surface. It was quiet, peaceful. In her confusion, she thought it might be nice to stay for a while. Then her bright orange life jacket forced her upward and she emerged from the river like a bass hitting a juicy fly. She fell backward and saw that her boat was a few yards away and that its driver steered it directly toward her.

Lance reached for the black handle on the back of her life jacket and swung her quickly into the boat. She landed at his feet, sputtering and coughing, an object of concern for the other boaters. Lance handed her a miraculously dry towel and she wiped her face, removed her helmet, and dabbed at her hair. The sputtering changed to giggles that blossomed into laughter, accompanied by tears.

She looked up at her rescuer, a dark image silhouetted against the afternoon sun. It occurred to her that he might have saved her life—a first, in her experience. What sort of a reward was called for, she wondered? It wasn't like tipping a maître d' in a restaurant, was it? She surprised herself by saying a sincere "thank you" to him as he reached out to retrieve the wet towel. "You'll be fine," he said. "We'll bail out the boat and sit in the warm sun, feeling the breeze from my river. We will all be dry in half an hour, just in time for the next rapids. Life on the river is good!"

They crested two more rapids, without incident, before pulling their boat onto a sheltered sandy cove for the night. A supply boat had arrived earlier, and neat rows of small tents stood along the sandy shore. Another guide managed an outdoor kitchen, offering cold drinks to the voyagers.

The man with the youthful girlfriend walked stiffly from the boat to the dining table. The girlfriend no longer looked at him with youthful ardor. The honeymooners quickly disappeared around a bend in the canyon wall, and the other travelers sat on campstools sipping cold beer. Tureen looked at the eddies and lappets on the river, which reflected late-afternoon sunlight like emeralds in a treasure chest, and lifted her gaze to the steep, multihued canyon walls reaching upward, framing the deep blue sky above.

She was happy and at ease, fully relaxed, soothed by the murmur of rushing water and songs of doves, killdeer, flycatchers, and blackbirds. She dozed, and then gently wakened to Lance's tap on her shoulder.

"Chow," he said. "Trout from the river, greens, sourdough bread, other stuff. You hungry?"

"Yes," she said, hoping the trout weighed a couple of pounds.

Tureen decided not to try sleeping in the open that night, although she marveled at the hazy brightness of the Milky Way directly above her. She stretched out her arms as though she could reach the stars. Contentment glowed within her. She crawled into her tent, moved her hips to conform the Adjustapad® to her body, and drifted off to blissful sleep.

The following evening, after a day of maneuvering through placid and swift currents and a handful of number three rapids, the travelers were again relaxing, looking at water birds frisking over a sandbar island a few yards from shore. Tureen enjoyed a frozen margarita made with powdered alcohol and frosted in a portable geothermal cooler. She felt smugly self-confident, having worked her way through the rapids that day without incident. From his position in the stern, Lance offered her smiles of encouragement, which she reciprocated brightly.

Now, after a meal of synthetic buffalo stew, biscuits, greens, beans, and a cold malt liquor the guides called "panther piss," Tureen was ready for what Lance called "shuteye."

"You know, I think I would like to try sleeping under the stars tonight," she informed the guide.

"Want me to help you find a safe spot?" asked Lance.

Yes, she did—she did indeed.

Lance scooped up her Adjustapad®, a blanket, and her inflatable pillow.

"There's a nice quiet spot around this bend. Good soft sand and palo verde bushes are in flower there. Yeah, nice spot. Straight-up view of the stars, too."

In twilight, they walked a few hundred yards from the main campsite along the sandy shore of the river to the nice spot, in a sandy cove surrounded by shrubs. Just yards from the rushing river, Lance began to set up her rustic bed. Bending to help him, Tureen's cheek brushed his, and she felt the stubby bristles rake her skin. It was strangely exciting.

Accidentally, it seemed, their lips met, soon followed by her left breast miraculously falling into the calloused cup of his hand. His rough thumb rubbed across her nipple, and it was as though her erect flesh had slipped into an active light socket. A sharp current of pleasure coursed down her spine and coalesced in a tender spot seven inches below her navel. In moments, they faced each other, shirtless and gleaming in the sparse moonlight, eager to explore the mysteries and delights of their bodies.

Lance leaned toward her and whispered, "Are you adventuresome?"

"Sure," she answered, curious, surprised.

"Ready to go for a triple orgasm?"

She nodded, breathless.

Lance reached out to unbuckle the wide belt holding up her Quickdri™ rafting pants.

"I like to start with a little spanking," he said.

She shivered in anticipation.

"Oooh,"whispered Tureen as she placed her hand on his, unclasping the buckle.

When she awoke, suffused with pleasure, and somewhat sore, Lance was gone. She yawned and stretched, letting the blanket slip aside, and inventoried the surface of her naked body in the misty morning light. Little raspberry marks showed on her inner thighs, and her scarlet pubic hair was matted and curled against her alabaster skin. Her breasts tingled as she recalled the night's explorations, and she smiled wistfully as she felt her buttocks throbbing as she shifted position.

Deciding it was time for a wash, Tureen pulled the blanket about her shoulders and walked into the river, splashing chill water over her tender parts. It felt wonderful, liberating. She dried herself with the blanket, retrieved her clothes, and walked slowly back to the main campsite. She watched the mist above the river catch the golden morning light, saw birds cruising along the mighty walls of the canyon, heard larks singing. Tureen was deeply in love with nature, suffused with wonder at her beautiful surroundings.

Of course, she thought, having had the best sex in years might be influencing my joy of this wonderful morning. But how, on God's green earth, could anyone want to sell off this incredible place? Her desire to defeat the Parks Act was rekindled, enhanced. She and Portia MUST prevail, by any means available. Under fresh resolve, she entered the campsite. Lance was there, pouring coffee for the others. He saw her arrive and offered a warm smile.

How crazy is this, she thought, as her heart seemed to leap from her throat. She couldn't recall ever yearning so much for a man.

The next night they repeated their carnal ballet, to resounding mutual acclaim. The raft trip ended the following morning, and the travelers departed amid insincere promises of keeping in touch and fussy little hugs. Tureen and Lance also embraced decorously, in strong contrast to their intertwined bodies of the night before, and Tureen pressed a note with her private fob code and some endearments into his hand. He slipped his braided horsehair bracelet on her wrist. They exchanged quiet vows of future meeting, but Tureen shed hot tears of loss as she climbed into the funicular to the south rim of the canyon. Of course, she would never see Lance again. Her eyes were still puffy and red when she met Portia and Grover.

DECISION TIME

Portia and Grover walked to a lookout on the south rim of the canyon to experience dawn playing across the multihued turrets of the canyon walls. They sat on a bench and marveled at the kaleidoscopic changes in the surrounding monuments with each passing minute. Tiny rainbows appeared in the mists clinging to the western walls. The somber river below displayed early-morning kayakers blinking like orange fireflies across the dark green expanse of water. A light updraft carried hawks and kestrels aloft, where they sailed effortlessly in the wind. Mesmerized, they watched the birds, the awesome topography of the canyon, the sun cresting the monuments in the east. They heard the sharp cries of the raptors and the rustle of green shrubbery caught in the morning breeze.

"Paradise," said Portia as she took a sip of coffee from a cardboard cup, which a raven perched on the bench next to them eyed greedily. Grover put his arm around her and hugged her shoulder. She rested her head in the crook of his neck and sighed.

"In that madhouse where we both work you forget there are places like this with such awesome beauty," she said.

Grover agreed. "I just wish we had more time to stay and enjoy all this, but there are urgent reasons why we have to get back." He glanced at her swollen stomach and reached across to give it a gentle pat. "Not the least of which is the future Merson down there."

Portia pulled away and sat up straight.

"Yes. That reminds me, we haven't talked about the chip yet. You always seem to change the subject."

"Perhaps you are right," Grover said. "Mainly it's that I just haven't made up my mind."

"We don't have much time. We need to decide."

The "chip" was a tiny receiver/transmitter half the size of a grain of rice designed to be implanted in the soft tissue beneath a baby's ear moments after birth. The chip monitored genetic characteristics, shifts in metabolism, rate of growth, weight, electrical brain wave activity, and dozens of other health metrics. It transmitted the collected data daily to recently installed receptors paired with existing fob towers where the yottabytes of data streamed to immense collection centers to be analyzed and recorded. Predetermined deviations from standard parameters within the health characteristics measured were flagged and reported to individuals or their designated health information receivers.

The chip had been available to parents on a voluntary basis for the previous four years. The results of its use were stunning. Infant mortality in the United States decreased by nine percent; early intervention reduced autism in children dramatically; prompt application of immunotherapy almost eliminated Ewing sarcoma among children. Consequently, the secretary of Health and Human Services recommended that the chip be mandatory for newborns beginning in the year after Portia's baby was born. Following the customary internecine battle about the unconstitutional use of executive privilege, Congress endorsed the secretary's recommendation. Portia and Grover had to decide whether the chip should be implanted in their new son.

"I get that the chip has fantastic abilities to alert medical professionals to health complications," said Grover, "but it also has GPS capabilities, among other things, that can tell 'authorities' where our son is for the rest of his life. With the abolition of the Affordable Care Act, insurance companies could deny coverage to people with illnesses reported by the chip. Employers might refuse to hire people with the potential for long-term medical problems. I don't know how secure all that medical information is. Just look at what happened last month when hackers downloaded those recorded fob conversations that were supposed to be highly secure. The news that two NFL fullbacks enjoyed wearing women's underwear ruined their careers. I have my doubts."

Portia shifted her weight on the bench and stared over the canyon before responding.

"You're right. We have to balance the possible invasion of his right to privacy against cutting-edge health care. It's like the risk we take every day in using our fobs. We know that there is a good chance that someone will monitor our use, but we use it anyway for all the benefits we gain. It's like not so long ago when people made unrestricted use of supposedly confidential emails and posted all sorts of personal information on social networks. People all over the world mined what they called the Internet and sucked up all that personal information, bundled it, and sold it to crooks, intelligence agencies, and employers."

Grover nodded. "It's a classical risk/benefit conundrum. We can figure out the risks, but how great are the benefits?"

"I think that observation is helpful," said Portia. "With all the new medical advances, and the ability to sequence our genomes in half an hour, doctors can figure out what ails us and prescribe a cure very quickly. Who's to say there won't be even greater advances, maybe even a cure for the common cold, during junior's lifetime? After all, the chip just alerts us when something goes wrong. It's not a cure."

"Good point. And no chip means junior won't always be on government radar," said Grover.

"Well…don't forget all the surveillance machines everywhere. I think there even are monitors located all along the rim of this canyon," said Portia, pointing toward a small glinting lens protruding from the base of a scrub pine.

"Still, our locations aren't instantly available to anyone who wants to know," Grover said.

"You're probably right. Anyway, I think we'll skip the chip—on the basis of individual freedom."

"Done!" said Grover.

The issue resolved, they gazed across the canyon at now brilliant red, orange, and ochre highlights painted on the massive monuments in front of them.

Coincidentally, a few weeks later, the National Civil Liberties Union adopted "Skip the Chip" as their battle cry to thwart the mandatory implantation of chips. They advocated civil disobedience and outright refusal on the part of parents to allow their babies to be "maimed." Law enforcement agencies reportedly planned to refuse to enforce the regulation. They envisioned headlines to the effect that police officers tore babies from their parents' arms to implant a "foreign object." Pediatric surgeons simply refused to touch the chip. Like many of President Hofnarr's innovative proposals, this was destined for a beltway orphanage where no congressperson admitted parentage, and an early grave.

Portia and Grover exchanged concerned glances as Tureen joined them in the timbered, high-ceilinged lobby of the lodge. Tureen seemed flushed and her eyes were puffy and red. Damp curls signaled that she had just taken a shower, and new freckles on her face and arms indicated long days of sunshine on the river. She ordered a Campari with vodka from an attendant as she settled in the fashionably worn leather chair next to her friends.

"Good time on the river?" asked Portia.

"Absolutely. Very beautiful and lots of fun. I only almost drowned once."

Tureen expanded on her adventure, enthusiastically describing the beauty of morning mists across the green waters, the excellent meals on the riverbanks, and the mostly nice people in the rafting group. There was, however, no mention of Lance Peppercorn. She did not want to discuss such a painful subject. Or risk getting emotional again. Crying in the shower was miserable enough.

Shifting the subject, she said brightly, "The experience on the river has invigorated me. I am more dedicated than ever to stopping the Parks Act—and I just learned from a fob check that we now have new ammunition. Have you been following the projections about what the 'TGT' means to the national economy?"

Portia and Grover were aware of the Tokamak Generator Tax, but had been so involved in enjoying their brief vacation that they had tuned their fob to deliver only personal messages.

"Sorry, we're only generally aware of the 'TGT,'" said Portia.

"Well," began Tureen, "the carbon based lobby persuaded Congress to create a 'level playing field' by creating a substantial national tax on electricity from Tokamaks to fund the significant corporate welfare they received from existing tax loopholes. Makes no sense, of course, but what else is new?"

Her friends offered grim grins to acknowledge that beltway fact of life.

"But the thing is," she added, "the GAO miscalculated. To satisfy the carbon lobby they designed the tax using a hypothetical carbon energy avoidance cost—the cost of energy two years ago, before the threat of cheap electricity dropped the value of a barrel of oil to less than twelve dollars. So, homeowners and businesses using Tokamak energy that costs almost nothing will have to pay Uncle Sam a use tax of two cents per kilowatt hour. Turns out that is much less that the Tokamak customers paid before, and will generate, over time, many trillions of dollars in new taxes, more than anyone expected from the sale of the national parks.."

"I guess I heard that just before we left on this trip," said Grover.

"So, how does this affect the Parks Act?" asked Portia.

"Well, out allies are pointing out that with all this new money coming in, why sell the parks? Many voters agree, since they suspect new money from the parks will be frittered away on half-assed projects. Remember the project to grow blue cheese on the moon, or the elevator to the stratosphere? We have an excellent new argument against the Parks Act here!"

"But not much time," noted Portia.

"We can do a lot in two or three weeks," said Tureen, "and we can employ Sneath Naydir to help, whether he likes it or not, and have another chat with your friend Melvin."

Benjamin Franklin Chang almost threw his fob against the wall after looking at Tureen's most recent message about the Parks Act. She said she understood his urgent need to secure one or more national parks, but an unexpected event, the imposition of the Tokamak tax, had "changed the landscape." She went on to explain that, in spite of her firm's best efforts, the new tax might change a few votes on the Parks Act. She had every confidence that, when the dust settled, he would be satisfied with the results.

"Lying bitch!" he exclaimed. Sylvester Chu, Esq. told him not an hour before that Tureen was promoting the TGT as an antidote against the Parks Act. He regretted being the bearer of distressing information.

"Distressing" doesn't half cover it, thought Chang. It was time to impose justice. Nobody got away with cheating Benjamin Franklin Chang—not ever. He motioned his fob to collect all known information, public and private, about Tureen O'Porto and created a comprehensive file that opened under a portrait of his intended victim.

Simple killing was too good for her. Something more dramatic was called for.

Dandy Fu's face appeared on the fob screen. One look at Dandy's perennially quizzical expression confirmed that he was not the tallest tree in the forest, but he was a loyal henchman who carried out Chang's orders unfailingly—so long as critical thinking and creativity were not involved.

"Chow, man," greeted Dandy. "Wassup, boss?"

Chang described Dandy's assignment. Dandy carefully recorded the details on his fob.

"So, that's like in Washington, the DC, right? Do I get to sit up front on the orbital to DC? So, that's a no—gotta stay in back. OK. You sure I can get sulfuric acid in stores over there? Sure. Put it on one of those plastic squirt bottles. Like for catsup. Like that. Got it, man."

As Chang's image dimmed, Dandy put down his fob and licked the tip of a pencil to prepare it for taking notes about his just completed conversation.

In a weekly ritual established many years earlier, Chang made a stop at the municipal police station to exchange pleasantries with Chief Inspector Arnold Fong before his appointment for a Thai body massage. Although the two men appeared to operate at opposite ends of the legal spectrum, they had been friends since childhood. They were further bound by a personal favor Fong provided in the past when he investigated the charred body of Yo Yo Farnsworth, the archrival of Chang's father and his reputed killer. The corpse had its feet nailed to the expensive teak floor of the living room in the deceased's mansion. Apparently, an accelerant enhanced the conflagration that destroyed the mansion.

Well versed in the criminal lore of his precinct, Fong knew that his child-hood friend would be a prime suspect in the death of this paragon of Hong Kong's crooked society. He managed to expunge all references to nailed feet and accelerants from his report. The official version of the event was that the unfortunate victim succumbed in a blaze started by absentmindedly dropping his lit cigar into a glass of 176-proof Balkan vodka.

They talked about family and mutual friends, reviewed football scores, and traded insults about Fong's expanding waistline and Chang's receding hairline. Then, rising to leave, Chang placed an envelope on his friend's desk.

"Just a little something for the Fong retirement fund—a continuing expression of my gratitude."

Quicker than yesterday, the envelope disappeared into a desk drawer.

"Completely unnecessary, but highly appreciated," said Fong, clasping his friend's hand warmly. "See you next week, I hope."

"Count on it," said Chang as he left his friend's office.

It was only a short walk from the municipal building to the ornate apartment house where the enterprising Mme. Fontainebleau, a Vietnamese expatriate, maintained her exclusive massage emporium. Chang walked briskly along the crowded streets, anticipating his body massage, where two charming young women rubbed aromatic oils over their naked bodies and massaged his body with theirs.

As Chang reposed on a massage table, the women began working on his toes and calves, moving upward. Departing from their customary approach, the women moved to his hands, and Chang felt them spray something cool and astringent on his palms. They then pulled his hands to the middle of his back and pressed his palms together. It was then that Chang smelled the pungent odor of medical Evrtite®, the ultra-adhesive that bonded skin in an instant. He was familiar with the product since he had used it to discipline underlings who acted badly. Surgery was the only way to separate bonded body parts.

Frightened and angry, Chang turned his head and said "Wha…" as a hard rubber ball was placed into his mouth and secured with nylon bands behind his head. Similar nylon straps secured his knees and feet until he resembled a pot roast tied with string. A terrified Chang wriggled atop the table until an unseen hand pinched his nostrils together, cutting off his air supply. He stopped wriggling and the hand relaxed.

He sat up and with wild eyes searched the room. The women were gone. Two unknown well-muscled men stood on each side of the table; at the foot stood someone he recognized.

Manchu Farnsworth, son of the community leader who had his feet nailed to an expensive teak floor at Chang's orders, stared at Chang with pitiless eyes.

"You are a snake in the grass," said Manchu. "Pretending to be a friend of the family, working together with my father, all the while arranging to have him killed. It took years for me to find you out, but now we know."

Chang tried to speak, but no words passed the rubber ball. Manchu gestured to the other men and a dark cloth bag descended over Chang's head.

When it was removed, Chang lay on the marble floor of the large bathroom in his own apartment.

"Good-bye, unspeakable filth," said Manchu as his men picked him up and deposited Chang in his large bathtub. He realized he was not alone. Smooth dry scales moved sinuously under his body. Like the exposed wires of a telephone cable, bushels of many colored pit vipers twined around his bound legs and arms. The vipers were on loan from the city's serpentarium, where Manchu had an important contact. Their pits are sensitive to temperature, and they seek out warm, moist spots.

His captors left the bathroom as one of the bushmasters began to explore the warm, moist spot between Chang's legs.

At the same time, Dandy Fu gazed out the window of his stratocruiser, looking at the blue sky below and the black, starry night above. He could make out the west coast of the United States below. In less than an hour, the cruiser would arrive at Dulles airport. He reviewed his notes from the conversation with Chang and stared at Tureen's image on his fob.

"Sneath," announced Tureen, "I need your help with Senator Horowitz."

So, thought Sneath, the other shoe has dropped. For weeks, he had wondered if Tureen would require his services in exchange for saving him from prison and, worse, as a drug dealer. He still experienced a sinking feeling in the pit of his stomach when he thought of sitting in the back of the police van, waiting to be carted off to the local precinct, and the relief he felt when Tureen told him to open the van door and go home. She was absolutely in her right to demand recompense. It was the way of the beltway. He simply wondered when the demand would come and what it would entail. Something to do with the crumbling 4-H Club, of which Horowitz was one of its two remaining members.

Senator Deborah Hatchett drummed Senator Hinckle out of the club when he decided to vote against the Parks Act. Ironically, Senator Hatchett now spent all her time preparing to defend herself against charges that her real estate company had bilked the government out of millions by applying affordable housing credits to constructing luxury penthouses. She had neither time nor interest in doing anything other than simply voting for the act.

Sneath pasted on his warm, friendly face and smiled at Tureen's image.

"Whatever you want, Tureen. How can I help?"

"With votes swinging away from the Parks Act because of the anticipated revenue flow from the Tokamak Tax, we need to reeducate senators who so staunchly supported the act. We think Horowitz is a good candidate, now that there is a legitimate excuse to scrap the Parks Act. You have been working with him for a long time. Any suggestions that don't involve money changing hands?"

Sneath understood that meant persuading the senator through reasoned argument or modest blackmail, otherwise known as "deal making." Since Horowitz had not engaged in reasoned argument in over a decade, Sneath knew that blackmail would be the order of the day. However, what unsavory element of the senator's seemingly upstanding years of service could he use?

"I understand your needs," said Sneath. "Just leave it in my hands for a day or so. I'll get back to you."

Sneath leaned back behind his desk, pushed both forefingers to his lips, and searched his inventory of the senator's positions and foibles. His vote against Israel's plan to turn southern Iran into an atomic wasteland was damaging, but only political. His plan to build a five hundred-year barrier against the rising waters of the East River only around the Green Point section of Brooklyn where his parents lived was damaging, but not fatal. Maybe something personal, closer to home. Sex…or money…or both.

Sneath positioned his fob so it could read his iris and open the most confidential files in his possession. He scrolled down the list of his Senate contacts, looking for the little red lightning bolt that signified critical information. Horn, Hornak…aah, Horowitz. There was a little red mark. He selected it and the words "likes boys and pork" came up. Finally, something to work with! He advised Tureen.

"Horowitz is in the bag. Wait until Wednesday."

Melvin Salmon was delighted to see Portia again. In his view, her expansive pregnancy only made her prettier. He found her slightly fuller cheeks and much fuller breasts more attractive than before. The lump of frustration just below his Adam's apple became almost painful. Finding her more desirable yet unattainable hurt. He sighed and turned his attention to the subject of their meeting..

"OK, I checked my sources on the way over," said Melvin. " I see that the gap between pro and con on the Parks Act is shrinking, but the odds are still three to two that the act will pass. It may be necessary for me to provide assistance."

"I agree. Our latest numbers say the vote will be close. With Senator's Horowitz' decision to scrap the act, however, there is a strong chance we will prevail," said Portia.

Tureen nodded. "The question now is: How do we orchestrate your help for the better good?"

"Let's see. The vote is scheduled for when—two days from now? I did a dry run. I can manage whatever is necessary from my fob, anywhere in the Capitol," said Melvin.

Portia resolved her moral dilemma before the meeting with Melvin. After her visit to the Grand Canyon, saving the national parks became more than a mission. It was an obsession. In this case, the ends would justify the means. Tureen, whose entire career was based on ends justifying means, suffered from no moral concerns. She was determined to win at all costs. Her Grand Canyon experience simply fortified her customary approach to issues like this.

"Can you tell me, Melvin, how it would work?" asked Portia.

"I've developed a little program that I can patch into the proper algorithm moments before voting on the Parks Act begins. You know that computers spend most of their time waiting for input from operators. This program will grab all the votes as they are created and do a real-time analysis of trends and project how many more 'nay' votes are needed to thwart the act. If votes need to be changed to affect the outcome it will occur automatically."

"Yeah," said Tureen, "but won't some senators know that their vote wasn't recorded properly?"

"Maybe not," said Melvin. They will all be looking at the 'big board' and wondering who voted for and against the act. As you know, what first shows up are the raw numbers. The specific voting information by state comes later. So when everyone is excited about how it turned out, things might be missed. Anyway, who is going to believe some senator who challenges our infallible system that cost the Senate so many millions? It will just be considered an ineffectual attempt to alter his original vote or sour grapes."

"So, this algorithm, will it tell **us** how the vote was changed?" asked Portia.

"That's the beauty part. You know I like games. This is my guessing game. The little program disappears once the vote is cast. We won't know whether it changed the vote or not."

"That's cruel!" exclaimed Portia.

"Not so," said Melvin. "You and I don't need to know, and what we don't know can't hurt us. What do they call it? Yeah—"plausible deniability." I'm doing us all a favor."

The two women silently considered Melvin's favor.

THE VOTE

On the day before the vote, Tureen sat at the desk in her glass-enclosed office overlooking the Mall. After hearing of Benjamin Franklin Chang's horrible and untimely death, she was reviewing recordings she made of their conversations and examining her original retainer contract. Each time she saw his lascivious image she recoiled involuntarily. The way his tongue moved as he licked his lips was serpent-like. How could she not think of his death by venom? That caused a brisk chill across her back, shoulders, and glands at the hinge of her jaw. She paused in her research and glanced out the window at brilliant sunshine on the Capitol building, making it chalk white against deep blue sky in stark contrast to the artificial lawn. She breathed a long sigh.

Just as she concluded that there were no loose ends in her relationship with Chang, her assistant's face materialized at the corner of her desk.

"There's, um, a person here to see you," he announced. "I don't recognize him, and he has no appointment. Says he's a friend. Should I bother to show you his Versalphoto[3]?"

"All right," said Tureen, suspecting it was either another luxury car salesperson or investment advisor. "Let me see."

---

3   Slang for "Universal Photo Identification," a document provided under sponsorship of the United Nations Authority and recognized as irrefutable proof of personhood.

It was Lance Peppercorn, sinewy arms protruding from a denim jerkin, pleasant smile on a bronzed face. The holographic image rotated in her view, and she caught her breath at the sight of his left earlobe, which she had used for erotic purposes not so many weeks ago.

"Oh, yes, please send him in," she said, patting her scarlet hair and smoothing her jacket.

She stood to meet him as he entered the room, and they exchanged a brief, self-conscious hug, long enough for her to notice his tangy aroma, long enough for him to feel her breasts against his chest. She gestured toward the corner of the office and they sat across from each other, smiling, a little shy, a little unsure of themselves.

"I'm so happy," she said. "I wasn't really sure when we would see each other again. I'm so happy you are here."

"You said in your note 'any time' and I took you at your word. Borrowed a friend's pickup, helped out a few hitchhikers trying to escape the famine, made it here in a little less than three days. Damn, woman, I'm very happy to see you, too. You got any place more private here perhaps?"

Of course. There was her private bathroom. She paused at her desk to click the "Do Not Disturb" button as she led her lover to the bathroom door.

Later:

"You remember the old joke about smoking after sex?" asked Tureen.

"Not sure. How does it go?" he answered

"The question is 'Do you smoke after sex?' and the answer is 'I don't know. I haven't looked.'"

"Oh, that's bad!"

"Maybe, but right now I think I'm smoking just a little bit," she said, rubbing his cheek.

"I'd better look," he said.

His fob flashed an inaudible alarm as the stratocruiser began its descent to the DC area. Dandy Fu transferred the urgent message to the Oculus device on which he was watching pornography. He deciphered the Mandarin calligraphy.

"Chang is dead. You are free to seek new employment. Details follow."

The message dissolved into a grisly picture of his former employer taken soon after his corpse was found in his bathtub. It represented proof of death, should there be any doubt on Dandy's part.

Complex feelings almost overwhelmed the little assassin. His eyes dampened at the thought of losing his generous employer, a man he held in such high regard that he would never lie to him unnecessarily. On a professional level, he wondered about the way Chang had been dispatched. Never had he seen such horror etched on a victim's face.

Then he began to worry about finding new employment with his narrow skill set. Never an apt student, Dandy was not current in modern techniques of human intelligence gathering and elimination. He was comfortable with pliers and a blowtorch, making holes in people, and landfill disposal. Even using acid was a reach for him.

His fee for the intended disfigurement of the O'Porto woman was in his account and a cash advance for expenses was secure on his fob. Since Chang was dead, no one could complain if he simply took in the capital sights and boarded a return flight to Hong Kong. There would be no need to deal with corrosive sulfuric acid, rubber gloves, and all that.

However, he made a commitment to a respectable criminal, had accepted a professional commission, and had received a fee he could not now return. He decided. Chang's unhappy departure did not alter his agreement. He would fulfill his obligation. It was the honorable thing to do.

That evening, in Tureen's apartment, Lance confessed that he had been in the area for almost a week, visiting friends in Maryland and Virginia and looking for work. He persuaded the manager of the exclusive Burning Bush Golf Club nearby in Maryland that he was just the man needed to supervise the club's large maintenance crew.

"There are more than fifty people on the crew," he reported, "and over fifteen acres of actual grass and woodland. Of course, the greens and fairways are all artificial, but they are maintained just like natural growth. My new boss was impressed with what he called my 'environmental awareness.' Seems the former supervisor let noxious runoff into the local streams and they had to pay a hefty pollution fine. And also restock the frogs, salamanders, and fish they killed."

"That seems to happen a lot," said Tureen. "Thoughtless and wanton disregard for our environment." My, she thought, this is the new me. How her visit to the Grand Canyon had changed her!

"No free lunch," noted her outdoorsman/oarsman. "Look at how we managed to melt the icecaps. We can grow palms along with cherry trees here, but we have to put floodgates in the Potomac to keep the Capitol basement from flooding."

Lance added two more inches of Barolo to their wine glasses.

"Anyway, this job isn't seasonal. Maintenance goes on all year, and the pay is in six figures. I'll be able to take you out to dinner every once in a while."

"I'll look forward to that," said Tureen. "Have you found a place to stay?"

"Colonial Arms garden apartments. Not too far away."

"That's nice," said Tureen, as she considered moving accumulated debris out of her guest bedroom.

Senator Pierre Rowe rejected the sergeant-at-arms' offer of a ride to his seat in an electric cart. He shuffled down the aisle using his cane more as a foil than a support, making comments and observations to friends on both sides of the aisle. Rowe had spent the last few days working to point out the asininities of the proposal made by senators supporting the Parks Act. Their scheme was to reduce the Tokamak Tax through amendment, thereby eliminating the surplus that made the anticipated funds from the Parks Act unnecessary.

Their plan codified long-standing conservative precepts: cut taxes and reduce the size of government. Rowe pointed out that adherence to those principles contributed to the nation's precarious economic situation and the parlous nature of the country's roads, bridges, and ports. Two days earlier he reminded Senator Hazard that cutting taxes simply meant cutting services, a fact that contributed to the Senate's negative approval rating.

"Negative approval rating?" barked Senator Hazard. "That sounds like a true lie to me! How can you support such a nefarious statement?"

Always prepared, Rowe's assistant projected the latest Pew survey on the large monitor above the chamber's speaker stands. In patriotic white, blue, and red graphics, the survey showed, with a three percent possibility of deviation, that the Senate's populace approval rating was a minus twelve.

Hazard grunted, "Pete, that's just like you. Trying to win an argument with biased facts. I refuse to accept this specious twaddle."

Hazard withdrew, allowing Rowe and others to create a deal about the Tokamak Tax.

A Senate vote in favor of forming a study committee to consider reducing the Tokamak Tax postponed the resolution of that issue. It also permitted some senators to report to constituents their strong support for reducing the tax. To achieve this result, the prevailing argument was that lack of action, or benign neglect, in moments of uncertainty is the wiser course.

The result was that on this morning the only item on the agenda was the up or down vote on the Parks Act.

Spectators packed the chamber. Reflecting the importance of the vote, only seventeen of the 102 members were present in holographic form. Eighty-five flesh and blood senators, an unusually high number, awaited the vote. Mini-drone cameras flitted about, capturing the images of numerous senators as they chatted with their colleagues and prepared to vote. Home monitors showed their faces; voting statistics; lifetime approval ratings by HRA, NRA, and NVA; family members; and previous political offices. A band of yellow letters scrolled under that information, showing the latest odds on the act's passage and the exhortation that it was not too late to place a bet.

The presiding officer banged her gavel and declared that debate was ended and that voting would proceed. She ceremoniously inserted her voting card into the receptacle before her, and looked up at the monitor on the wall behind her. There was one vote in favor of the act.

In Tureen's office, she, Portia, and other members of her firm watched the Senate proceedings on the opaque wall of the room that also served as a monitor. They were able to distinguish the holographic from actual senators by their fuzzy blue outlines on the monitor. The mini-drone cameras captured in fine detail images of the senators sliding their voting cards into the receivers on their desks. Tureen and Portia wondered if Melvin Salmon's program was activated, whether it would work, whether it would be needed.

Dandy Fu placed his fob in translation mode as he entered the Fair Value Hardware Emporium behind DuPont Circle. He had an older application that did not provide simultaneous translation; a delay was involved after he spoke before the native language reached the ear of his listener.

He walked to the counter, held up his fob, and spoke to the counterwoman.

"I would like to purchase the acid used for the battery," he said.

"You got one of them old lead/acid jobs, huh? Don't get much call for them. But, yeah, we carry that in stock. It comes concentrated. How much ya need?"

"Lead acid? That is wrong. I want sulfur that is acid. Use in battery from olden days. It is corrosive, so I think," explained Dandy.

"Gotcha. We call it sulfuric acid here. How much ya need?"

"Half a liter, I suppose."

The woman pressed some buttons on her tablet, and a creaky, battered robot unfolded from a box on an aisle behind her and clanked away, soon returning with a bright red Teflon canister, which it deposited next to her on the counter.

"Anything else? Converters, plugs, fluids? What kinda old car you got anyway?"

Dandy listened carefully to his fob and looked confused. He moved a finger to repeat the translation, then consulted the fob for a response.

"Ford Edsel. My old car is."

"Naw. Never heard of it. That comes to eighty-seven dollars. I skipped the change."

Dandy transferred the money and carried the container of acid away in a cellulose microfiber sack. His next stop was a convenience store, where he purchased a squirt-top catsup bottle with "Heinz 74 Varieties" emblazoned on it, a pair of rubber gloves, and a funnel.

He finished flushing the catsup from his Heinz container down the drain in his hotel bathroom, carefully rinsed the bottle, and practiced squirting clear water through its nozzle at objects in the room. Soon there were puddles on the floor, and hand towels and toilet paper rolls were sodden.

This is not as easy as I expected, he thought. It took practice to exert the correct hand pressure to expel the stream of water at the needed velocity. Then there was the matter of aim. He always seemed to hit low. He practiced most of the morning until he was satisfied with his technique. He could hit the towel hanging from the rack exactly in the center almost all the time.

He went out to purchase two Turk-a-fillet™ sandwiches. He nibbled on one and placed the other in the bathroom sink, removing the sesame seed bun to expose the gray surface of the fowl meat. He pulled on rubber gloves, used the funnel to carefully decant the acid from its container into the Heinz bottle, and screwed on the nozzle tip. He upended the catsup bottle and let a few drops of acid hit the surface of the meat. Rotten egg odor hit his nostrils as steam rose from the dissolving meat, the acid etching a path to the sesame seed bun below, then the sink.

That's really fast, thought Dandy. Very effective. I better wear the rubber gloves. He carefully replaced the plastic tip on the nozzle of the Heinz bottle and placed it in a case designed for beer cans.

The morning's exertions had tired him. He considered taking a nap before turning to his next task: locating the office where Tureen worked.

Yellow flashing lights, reminiscent of fireflies, on the large monitor seemed to show exasperation with the slowness of the vote. Even now, some of the older senators paused to reconsider which of the four ways their voting card should be inserted in the voting slots on their desk. Most were able to distinguish the large red arrow showing the way, but some confusion remained. The sergeant-at-arms adjutants helped where they could.

The customary murmur in the chamber died out just after the presiding officer slammed down her gavel, and all eyes, chamber and gallery, focused on the large monitor. In seesaw fashion, the numbers on the aye and nay columns changed with each passing second. Pete Rowe glanced up to the gallery, where he saw Wylie watching the monitor with all the other visitors. He caught his eye, and Wylie offered a hopeful "thumbs up" signal.

The monitor showed eighty-seven votes cast: forty-six ayes and forty-one nays. Sensing victory, Deborah Hatchett offered gloating smiles to her supporters, many of whom were doing sums in their heads, estimating profits that lay ahead.

As the seconds ticked on, the smaller yellow column of nay votes began to grow. Forty-nine, fifty, fifty-one. It grew past the aye column and settled in at fifty-four. **Fifty-four**! The Parks Act was defeated. Cheers and applause filled the chamber, washing over the sour faces of those members who were certain the act would pass.

They craned their necks, searching for defectors. Implicit in their search was the fact that solemn promises of support were often broken when votes were cast. Only later would yea or nay votes be assigned to individual members. As Melvin Salmon predicted, senators who believed their votes had been recorded incorrectly were reluctant to complain. It would be embarrassing to admit they might have inserted their voting card in the wrong slot of the foolproof system. It would be equally upsetting to have their peers suspect they were lying about their vote to avoid political repercussions.

Not for a moment did anyone suspect an error in the voting system. Like the Senate itself, it represented the best program money could buy.

Portia and Tureen, ecstatic about the outcome of the vote, banished any thoughts about vote tampering. They hugged, a bit awkwardly, considering that Portia looked like a milkweed pod about to burst, laughed, and cried at the realization that all their efforts bore fruit. Soon, they were overwhelmed with congratulatory messages. Except, of course, from those of Tureen's clients who had paid for a different outcome. Tureen decided to deal with them tomorrow. Now it was time for celebration. The western governors proposed a victory dinner at the new Plume. Significant others were included. Tureen contacted Lance as Portia called Grover. It would be a splendid evening.

Before dimming the monitor, they watched the leader of the Senate offer her comments at an impromptu press conference.

"Of course I'm disappointed. I had every expectation that we would win. It was a fair fight, but I think the unexpected impact of the Tokamak Tax results swayed the vote away from us. We still believe that bolstering our economy with funds from the parks was and is a solid idea. It was a noble effort and I'm sorry it failed. Now I'm going to caucus with a lime rickey, and not take any more questions."

All of the more than five hundred "all news, all the time" broadcasters over the nation's more than four hundred million fobs reported the stunning defeat of the Parks Act. Talking heads from all colors of the political spectrum pontificated on the obvious and dissected every element of this seminal event. A tsunami of blather submerged rational intercourse. By the end of the week, comments about the Parks Act trickled away as new news about the discovery that humans shared a genome with the common garden slug poured into the nation's fobs.

Agatha Jackson fielded many requests for appearances on newstreams and gained instant celebrity when she appeared in full national parks uniform, including the cavalry campaign hat, to highlight plans to revitalize the parks, now that the threat of their sale was over. Senators also crowded the airwaves, happy to take credit for saving the nation's patrimony, blithely ignoring the fact that they had been longtime supporters of selling the parks.

Attendance at the national parks increased in the months before it seemed likely they would be sold. After the act was defeated, a kind of national sense of relief developed, and visits to the parks skyrocketed. Like someone escaping a death sentence who savored life all the more, the massive publicity about all the parks encouraged people to discover what they might have missed. Lines of couples waiting to be married among the massive trees of Muir Woods stretched along the roads leading to the park's entrance. The parks' administration established lotteries to select winter wanderers at Yellowstone. Americans waited for years to reserve visits to all the northeastern parks during foliage season.

So popular became the parks that the administration after President Cruz acceded to pressure from all sides to increase the national parks' acreage. Now that Alaska was enjoying much milder temperatures, and energy entrepreneurs were abandoning off-shore and on-shore drilling, vast areas of the state were added to the parks' roster. The Brooks Range and sites north of the Arctic Circle became well-attended summer recreation areas.

Melvin Salmon observed these proceedings from his private workroom, surrounded by many monitors that he regarded as background music, as he worked on his latest software application, simulated space flight to the planet of Nirvana. As one of the talking heads exhausted reason and theorized about a foreign conspiracy by Jesuits to thwart the Parks Act, Melvin paused in his work and chuckled. If you only knew, he thought. If you only knew.

A happy Wylie met with Pete Rowe in his office after the vote. Senator Rowe waved caution to the winds and enjoyed the first bourbon and branch in many years.

"Damn, Wylie, that's good," he said. "Can't think of a better occasion to confound that damn doctor's advice. I must confess, that vote had me going for a minute or two. I saw Deb Hatchett make her victory smirk and got concerned. Wonderful how the voting shifted at the last minute."

He reached across to clink Wylie's glass.

"Here's to the glories of democracy. Flawed as it may be, every once in a while it rears its lovely head and does the right thing. Today was a good day."

The two old friends sipped their drinks in contented silence. Wylie had congratulated Portia, telling her how proud he was of her, and now planned to offer his appreciation to his best friend, the white-haired senator sitting across from him.

He touched Rowe's arm. His friend clutched his glass tightly and looked at Wylie.

"Damn arm hurts like a mother bear. Hurts like…," he said as he dropped his glass and let his arm drop, slipping to his side, his head rolling toward his shoulder, a bewildered look in his pale blue eyes.

Wylie moved quickly to his side, called for his assistant just outside the door, supported his friend by holding his shoulders, watching, feeling him diminish in his arms.

"Wylie," said Senator Pierre Rowe as the light faded from his eyes.

"Goddamit, Pete," said Wylie, feeling helpless, tears falling.

LABOR DAY

T ureen, Portia, Grover, and Lance exited through the high glass doors of Tureen's office building and moved south along K Street. They all felt the results of the previous night's celebration, slightly hung over but still euphoric about their sparkling victory over the Parks Act. However, their current destination—the memorial service for Senator Pierre "Pete" Rowe—cast a pall over the group.

Portia was most affected. She had known her grandfather's friend all her life. Whenever they met, he treated her with great affection and, when she began to work in the Capitol, he opened many doors for her. Portia had been fascinated at the bond between the senator and her grandfather and the powerful friendship that lasted more than sixty years. She felt sorry that her grandfather had lost his best friend. Intimations of mortality caused her to think sadly about losing Wylie as well.

The others joined her for moral support, but Grover was particularly interested in staying close to his wife. Since she waddled like a Canada goose carrying a Calabasas squash, he was convinced his son would make his appearance at any moment. They walked together down the street, holding hands. Tureen and Lance walked behind them, his arm around her waist.

As they paused to cross the street, a small Asian man wearing goggles and dressed in a raincoat approached them. Apparently, the goggles obscured his vision, since he raised them to his forehead to peer at their group. His gaze intensified as he recognized Tureen with her flaming hair.

Lance observed this curious person and smiled as he incongruously pulled a catsup bottle from a pocket of his raincoat. Lance's first thought was: Is he looking for French fries or a hamburger on K Street?

He turned to Tureen to share his joke when his amusement turned to alarm. As he came closer to Tureen, the little man, holding the catsup bottle in hands protected by yellow rubber gloves, pointed the nozzle of the bottle directly at Tureen's face. Lance saw him squeeze the bottle, but nothing came out. The cap on the nozzle remained firmly attached.

Tureen quickly jumped back from her would-be attacker, and Grover, recognizing danger, moved in front of Portia, putting himself between her and the man in the raincoat.

As the little man tried to pull off the nozzle cap with his clumsy, rubber-encased hands, Lance jumped forward and pushed the hand that held the catsup bottle down toward the Asian's middle, pressing him forward so he fell on his face. Lance leaped on top of the attacker, pinning him to the sidewalk with his weight, holding his head by both ears, grinding his nose and forehead into the concrete. The man began to groan, then uttered a high-pitched screech, which Lance did not expect. The pitiful screech, like a mortally wounded forest creature, continued without pause. Surprised, and believing no more danger could come from the little man, Lance stood, allowing him to roll onto his back.

Dandy Fu stared dimly through his goggles at the office buildings surrounding him, the gathering crowd of onlookers, and the white-faced woman he tried to attack. Moaning, he threw aside the empty catsup bottle he had unwillingly clutched to his groin. Lance's body weight on his back as he lay prone had popped off the nozzle cap and expelled the acid in the general direction of his privates. In seconds, that area burned with the fury of a dozen jilted mistresses. He smelled sulfur and visualized dissolving flesh. The pain and the imagined dissolution of his cherished parts were too much to bear. His mind and body conspired to relieve him of his torture. He panted quickly for a moment or two and slipped into a coma.

Lance looked down at the little Asian man, begoggled, still wearing rubber gloves and a crumpled raincoat, mouth open and lifeless. It looked as though he had wet himself, except that a light sulfurous haze rose from the wet area, as did a bubbling sound like a teapot about to boil.

"Jesus!" Lance said, and prodded him with a toe, which produced a twitch in the man's right leg.

"He's not dead. I'll fob a Mergycopter for this poor bastard. What on earth was going through his mind?" said Lance as he hit the alarm button on his fob.

Curious rubberneckers surrounded the four friends and the small body curled up on the sidewalk. In a city accustomed to bloodless combat, the sight of a person suffering an actual injury was a novelty. Human nature being what it is, even those who saw Lance call for the Mergycopter used their fobs to duplicate the call. It was like the arrogance of those who rush forward to press an already lit elevator button. Their participation is required to validate the needed action.

The crowd thinned a bit as a white helicopter arrived, sending debris from the street and sidewalk swirling. It hovered above a median strip before slowly settling near the crowded walkway. Two emergency medical attendants carrying white satchels rushed into the crowd, to the little man. One pressed a medifob to his neck, read the digital information, and offered a thumbs-up sign to his companion, who inflated a carbon fiber stretcher and set it next to their patient. They quickly donned respirators and gloves, preparing to take the injured man to the helicopter.

Tureen, holding Lance's arm, and Portia, nearby, distanced themselves from the activity that swirled around them to consider their current conditions.

After moments of disbelief and denial, Tureen came to grips with the fact that someone had tried to attack her physically, that she had narrowly escaped disfigurement or worse. With eyes dilated and feeling overstimulated from the adrenalin that coursed through her, Tureen shivered at the thought of what might have been. She worked hard to hold back the trickle of vomit that pushed against the back of her throat.

Lance wondered what her attacker had on his mind, but Tureen thought she knew. This reeked of Chang's handiwork. Some of her contacts warned her about Chang's sometimes-fatal problem-solving techniques when she considered accepting him as a client. Only half believing the warnings and certain she could handle all comers, she added him to her client list. Only later, as stories about her client filtered in from many fronts, did she understand how murderous the leering little bastard could be.

A chill crossed the back of her neck. She had committed folly. She had ignored the best advice of friends and business associates, disregarded the sour feeling in the pit of her stomach each time she fobbed Chang, overlooked the ominous leer he presented during their last conversations. And then, she thought, I blithely played him against other clients. Chang wasn't stupid; he must have discovered she was working for the governors. Not that I deserve a physical attack, but I have no one to blame but myself, she thought dejectedly.

In her emotional pain, she looked at Lance, who held her close as she supported herself on his arm. He saved me again. Just stepped forward and put that little man down, as casually as hailing a Selfer®. She clutched his arm more tightly, looking at the tan and white crinkles in the corners of his eyes. But, before mushy affection settled in, she had another thought.

Were there any other little men in raincoats who had her in their sights? Chang was dead, but his orders could live on. She felt weakness in her legs, an urgent desire to sit down, a dryness in her mouth.

"I think, I think I need to sit down. Can we move through these people to the bench over there?"

Lance shouldered his way through the press of people surrounding the helicopter rescue and led her toward a bench near the Selfer® stop. As they neared the edge of the crowd, Tureen saw Portia laughing and leaning on Grover's shoulder.

"Portia, what's going on?" Tureen demanded.

As Grover gallantly jumped in front of Portia to protect her from the odd Asian attacker, his sudden movement put Portia off balance and she began to follow her belly as it slowly fell to the curb. Concentrating on the activity before him, Grover failed to notice that his wife had dropped out of view.

Feeling no urgent need to rise, Portia made herself as comfortable as possible and watched the drama of the attack and subjugation of the little man in goggles who writhed on the pavement just a few feet away. Suddenly she sensed that something had changed, that something had shifted in her burgeoning middle. Involuntarily she spread her legs and discovered wetness—not moisture, but a puddle of clear liquid—soaking her clothes and spreading on the pavement near her feet.

Whoa, she thought, this is it. My water broke. My God! I'm going to have a baby.

As she looked up, searching for Grover, she felt another new sensation, a clutching, a compression, like many hands trying to grasp a basketball in free play. Except the basketball was her baby, who objected to this rude push. She felt a diffuse pain that enveloped the place below her navel. Portia drew an involuntary sharp breath that eased the pain a bit, letting her relax. As she began to breathe more easily, the helicopter arrived and the medical team rushed to the immobile little man on the pavement nearby. Distracted by this new activity, the painful sensation diminished and disappeared.

So that's a contraction, she thought. I can handle that.

The oxytocin hormone along with other hormones generated during labor were beginning to course through her body at about three times the normal rate. Portia had an unobserved genetic glitch that caused her pituitary gland to secrete oxytocin in abnormally large amounts. Although harmless, this condition produced powerful contractions leading to a quick delivery, and feelings of well-being and intense affection. Portia was on the cusp of a speedy delivery and suffused with a hopelessly romantic love of all humankind.

"Poor little gangster," she mumbled as Dandy Fu passed her on a stretcher bound for the helicopter.

"Oh, Grover, darling," she cried as her husband found her still sitting on the curb and reached down to cradle her shoulder. She raised her arms to him, allowing him to pull her to her feet.

"My water broke and I've had my first contraction. No question about it, junior is about to come out. Ha ha! The noise from that helicopter must have been a wakeup call." She chortled. "And the go bag is at home. Yep, it's at home. *Tant pis.*[4]"

---

4   Portia minored in French. "*Tant pis*" means "so much the worse; too bad."

She reached both hands around her belly and said, "See you soon, baby. Hope everything comes out all right!" She laughed at her joke.

Grover had mixed feelings. Elated that the delivery of his son was at hand, and confused and concerned that his wife had become a happy drunk, he supported her as she leaned on his shoulder, humming a little tune.

Answering Tureen, Portia said, "I just went into labor. It's really interesting. Whoops! Here comes another contraction." She pointed to the upper part of her belly, shook her hands in mock fright, and made a scary face.

All thoughts of Chang's postmortem revenge evaporated and, sharing Grover's concern, Tureen said, "Portia, you're acting weird and we've got to get you to maternity." Grover remembered the maternity drill. He called a copter, pressed the fob button that alerted Portia's gynecologist to her status and location, and entered the key for the maternity ward where they had reserved her room.

Just after the medivac helicopter lifted off, the large white hospital copter arrived. Grover, Tureen, and Lance helped Portia through its portal and sat together as the craft lifted off.

"Oh, the Lincoln, Jefferson, and Eisenhower Memorials look so beautiful today, this beautiful sunny day, this nice sunny day...oh yes! Here comes another contraction. Whoopee."

The other three passengers looked at each other. What on earth was going on?

THE BABY, THE PIG,
AND THE ISLAND

"Popped out like a champagne cork on New Years," announced the nurse in the delivery room as she suctioned mucus from the baby's mouth and nose. The future scion of the Merson dynasty cried lustily as soon as his airways were clear, a loud, penetrating howl that testified to fortitude and character, or so Grover thought. Portia, still high on self-produced oxytocin, beamed at the freshly cleaned reddish lump delivered to her breast and marveled at the finely formed little fist that pushed into her skin.

"So perfect," she said. "Look at that. He even has tiny fingernails. And hair. Dark hair."

Portia turned to the nurse with a worried look.

"What about his eyes? Is something wrong? Why can't I see his eyes?"

"Honey," said the nurse, "that baby has been in your warm and dark belly for nine months. Now he's exposed to bright lights and noise. No wonder he keeps them shut. They'll be open in a few days and you will see his beautiful blue eyes."

"Blue eyes? You know they will be blue?

"They all start out blue or gray. You won't know his true eye color for about nine months. But dark hair and blue eyes would be very smart," said the nurse.

This was all news to Grover, who stood by the bed and examined his son. He was still recovering from accepting the nurse's offer to cut his son's umbilical cord. This practice was designed to permit the father to participate actively in the process of birth. The nurse clamped the cord and gave him scissors.

"But, won't it hurt?" he asked, fumbling with the scissors.

"I don't think so," said the nurse, "but it must be done. I'm sure he won't hold it against you. Just cut it right here."

Which he did, slicing the gray cord, feeling queasy as it parted, proud that the baby did not even flinch. Further evidence, thought Grover, of bravery and character.

"Um, does he get circumcised now?" asked Grover.

"Heavens no!" exclaimed the nurse. "That barbaric practice ended a couple years ago when Johns Hopkins confirmed that it deadened sensation at the tip of the penis, decreased lubrication, and lessened male sex drive. Remember how quickly Congress passed bipartisan legislation in response? And all those religious discrimination cases funded by rabbinical groups? Remember the thousand-mohel march on the Capitol?"

Grover wished he had not asked. He leaned toward his glowing wife and new son. He was intensely happy. Portia, still suffused with oxytocin and joyously itemizing every crease and hillock of her child, looked up at Grover.

"Just look what we made. Isn't he wonderful?"

Of course. Of course, thought Grover, who pressed his face to Portia's cheek and his son's smooth head.

Two floors below, in a security ward, Dandy Fu looked from his manacled wrist to the gaggle of green-clad doctors surrounding his bed. Groggy from painkillers, he fought through verbal fog, trying to understand what they were saying, why they seemed so excited. Listening through the tinny speaker from the group translator placed by his ear was difficult, and watching the large doctor's mouth move made him queasy. He tried to raise his arm to gesture for them to speak more slowly, but strained his wrist instead. Suddenly remembering what had happened after he tried to disfigure Tureen, he shut his eyes, ignored the voices around him, and reached with his free hand to the place between his legs.

He encountered a large bandage over raw flesh, smooth-seeming skin. No protuberance, no lumps, no sensation other than pressure. Confusion changed to realization. He turned his head and vomited what little remained in his stomach on to the crisp white pillow.

"That's all right. That's all right," said the large doctor. "Probably a reaction to the medicine we've been pumping into you. Nausea is a common side effect. But it does a fine job of reducing your pain. How are you feeling?"

"You crazy?" asked Dandy Fu. "I feel like death, like horror. How you feel without a joy stick[5]?"

The doctor smiled in acknowledgement, a very inappropriate thing to do in Dandy Fu's opinion. On top of everything else, he was beginning to have murderous thoughts about this white devil in a green smock.

"No laughing matter," he managed.

"Certainly not," said the doctor as those around him nodded in solemn agreement. "We fully understand your concern, and we want to review some exciting prospects for your recovery."

The doctor moved closer to the patient, like a conspirator, and purred his question.

"What would you say if I told you we can fix you good as new?"

"Not believe it," answered Dandy Fu. "You make me angry."

"It is true, though. We have had remarkable results with xenografts in cases like yours."

The translator searched for the correct Mandarin word for "xenografts." Finally, Dandy Fu heard "animal-to-human organ transplants."

He brightened.

"Animal? What animal? Lion? Bear? Horse?" he asked.

A group smile wreathed the faces of the doctors. The larger doctor said, "No. The most appropriate and most human animal for xenografts is a pig."

"PIG? Pig," said Dandy Fu, in deep despair again.

"Yes, I am afraid so. You must understand that this is an enormously elegant procedure…"

---

5   This was the closest the translator could come to the colloquial Mandarin for penis. Guïtóu literally means "turtle head."

Dandy Fu held up his free hand to indicate he did not understand what "elegant procedure" meant.

"What we do is harvest some of your stem cells that we turn into a human embryo, which we coax into the genesis of an organ—genitalia in your case. Since it originated from your own cells, your body is less likely to reject the new organ."

Dandy Fu dimly followed the doctor's description. He recalled a cloud story beamed onto his fob about clones that duplicated themselves to become an avenging army. What the doctor said must be true. But, how was a pig involved?

"In early days," the doctor went on, "we implanted the baby organ in the womb of the host animal, where the organ grew to maturity. Unfortunately, we had to kill the host animal to remove the fully formed organ before implanting it in a human. Now, however, we are able to place the growing organ externally on our host pig so that many organs are cultured simultaneously." The doctor suppressed a laugh. "You should see some of the pigs growing breasts, feet, noses, and genitalia. Very amusing."

Dandy Fu tried to erase his mental image of such a pig. He thought he might vomit again.

He had a question.

"How long does it take to grow that part?"

"Since the original parts were quite small, I think it would be a matter of three or four months. I wish we could improve upon nature, but we will be working with your stem cells," said the doctor.

Was it necessary to make that information public, thought Dandy Fu? However, he was relieved at the prospect of becoming whole again.

"Good," he said. "When do I begin?"

"We have taken the liberty of harvesting your stem calls already, on the possibility you might not survive your accident. Since you are recovering well, we can probably do the implant in a few months at the prison hospital."

"Prison hospital?"

"Oh, yes," said the doctor. "I have it on good authority that you will be spending quite a few years there."

Senator Deborah Hatchett stood atop the wall surrounding the medieval city of Dubrovnik, looking across the harbor to islands on the Adriatic coast. The daily press briefing issued by her staff reported that she was in the third day of an "information gathering" junket to review United States investments in relief camps for the trickle of immigrants still trying to escape the aftermath of the tripartite conflict between Hungary, Serbia, and Bosnia Herzegovina.

In fact, the senator did not intend to return from the "Pearl of the Adriatic." She planned to use her fortune to become an expatriate in Croatia and enjoy the fruits of all her labors.

As she enjoyed the balmy September day, watching waves break against the southern parapets of the city wall and boats bobbing in the sheltered harbor, Senator Hatchett complimented herself on her well-planned departure from Washington. It was orchestrated to avoid the bother of a federal indictment charging massive fraud. HUD, apparently, was peeved that her real estate company had diverted funds designated for affordable housing to penthouses and luxury condominiums.

Her careful research disclosed that Croatia had never signed an extradition treaty with the United States. Panoramic views of countryside and lush villas near Dubrovnik further persuaded her to consider the country as a safe, comfortable haven. Since she had prudently transferred large amounts of money by PayPal to a discreet bank account in Monaco, she had no financial worries.

The day before, she had looked at luxury villas and apartments on the hillsides of the modern city. They overlooked the harbor for cruise ships and yachts, with ocean views and quick access to the Adriatic highway across a large single pylon bridge. Compared with DC, prices were cheap and good help seemed readily available.

That evening, as she finished her meal in the Hotel Kazbek, a waiter announced she had a visitor waiting in the dark-wood paneled lobby. Curious but wary, she discovered a well-dressed, short, round, bald man sitting on an easy chair in the lobby, chatting with the assistant manager.

He rose quickly as she entered, beamed an enormous smile in her direction, and moved clumsily toward her.

"Oh, Senator Hatchett, such a great pleasure to meet you," he said, bowing slightly to reveal his glistening pate.

"Do I know you?" she asked.

"Alas, it is my great misfortune that I have until now not had that pleasure. I am Dominick Desiderato, at your service," he said, offering a square business card.

Amused at the formal words that came out of this man who resembled a well-dressed sloth, she read the engraved card.

Dominick Desiderato
Realtor of your Dreams
Fob—017ParadiseFound (727-23473-363)

"So, you're a realtor. I know something about that business. What do you want with me?"

"Madam, in all humility I confess that I am the best, most exclusive real property confidant of the expatriate community in Dubrovnik and its environs. My practice is limited to English-speaking persons, among whom I include Americans. The broker with whom you visited various villas today suggested I call on you. Did you not say something about a summer place on an outlying island where you could avoid the tourist crowds from the cruise ships?"

"That was really a joke," said the senator. But she was intrigued by this little man with the peculiar accent who must have swallowed the Oxford English Dictionary.

"No, it was very wise," he said." Our beautiful city is best enjoyed during the months surrounding the tourist season. That is when you make paramount use of your villa in town. The best people leave in July and August and enjoy the delights of the country in luxury cottages. It so happens that I have exclusive access to luxury cottages on Mljet Island, a short ferry ride from here. It would be my great pleasure to be your host for a fine lunch and visit to these exclusive and specially priced mini-villas."

Desiderato painted colorful word pictures of the delights of Mljet Island, interspersed with outrageous flattery concerning her lofty political position, her astonishing beauty, and impeccable good taste. Completely familiar with this technique, which she had used herself in the past, Senator Hatchett nevertheless succumbed.

Desiderato arranged to meet her at midmorning in the old city. He suggested a location with an excellent view of the city and the sea, and promised to be her guide through the ancient streets before taking the ferry to Mljet.

She arrived early to climb the ancient walls surrounding the city and enjoy a bird's-eye view of the crooked, narrow streets and glistening Adriatic. She was relishing the sweet morning air, listening to the cries of gulls swooping along the highs from the green-blue sea when Desiderato awkwardly pushed his bulk up narrow steps to join her.

"A lovely day, is it not, Senator?" Desiderato asked, dabbing his bald head with a linen handkerchief. "From here, we can look straight down the broad Placa to Orlando's Column. See the little harbor behind it? It is now early enough to enjoy an uncrowded walk along the main road, which is impossible after the tourist busses disgorge their passengers."

They descended the stone stairway to the main avenue together and strolled past shops, art galleries, and cafés. Morning breezes caught her green dress and she became almost giddy with feelings of lightness and pleasure at her surroundings. The place was as far from her troubles in the Capitol as she could imagine. She watched fishing boats bob in the little harbor and sunlight glistening across the sea, sharpening the outlines of the little islands to the south.

"Can one see Mljet from here?" she asked.

"No. That island lies to the north." He glanced at a pocket watch. "Actually, we need to get on our way to the ferry now. You can always return to the old city any time during your stay here."

Desiderato guided her to the taxi stand at the Pile entrance to the city, where he selected a comfortable Tesla sedan for the brief ride to the harbor on the north side of the modern city. There the ferry to Bari nosed against the highway to receive hundreds of vehicles that stretched up the roadway on the bluffs overlooking the sea.

The real estate agent helped Senator Hatchett from the taxi and directed her along the asphalt causeway leading to the covered passenger gangway that rose from the pier to an entrance above. Not yet loaded, the ship rode high in the water, exposing the rust-colored sides below the waterline.

"I didn't realize the ferry to Mljet was so big. It's like an ocean liner!"

"Well, of course it is," said Desiderato. "It just makes a stop at Mljet for additional passengers bound for Bari, which makes it convenient for those of us bound for that island. Then it crosses that Adriatic to the port of Bari on Italy's east coast. Depending on the weather, the trip takes less than ten hours. On a lovely day like today, I'd say the trip would take about eight hours."

"And how long to Mljet?" she asked.

"Less than an hour, dear lady," said he, offering her his arm as they ascended the gangplank.

The crew efficiently loaded all vehicles and passengers and, less than half an hour after they boarded, whistles and horns sounded their departure. Massive thrusters pushed the ship out of the harbor and turned it to a southwesterly course toward Italy. Senator Hatchett and her guide sat in the top deck lounge, where Desiderato persuaded her to join him in a glass of Lillet Rose. It was a perfect day: bright, smooth ocean; crystalline blue sky; fluffy clouds grazing the horizon like lazy sheep. As the ship slipped through the crisp green water, it began to pass a large, emerald island two miles or so off its starboard side.

Setting her drink down, she asked, "What island is that?"

"That is Mljet. Lovely place, is it not?" he replied.

"But, we aren't slowing down. Looks like we are going past it."

He leaned toward her across the table, placing his hand over hers.

"Just so. I haven't been completely honest with you. This ferry is nonstop to Bari. In Italy."

Her face registered confusion, eyes wide, mouth drawn down, followed by dawning awareness that something was seriously wrong. She stiffened, staring angrily at the little man across the table from her, pulling her hand away, grasping the edge of the table as though to hurl it at him. She felt a hand on her shoulder.

Another man who had been sitting nearby leaned into her line of vision.

"Senator Hatchett, I am Agent Dan Friendly," he said, "and this gentleman (he gestured toward Desiderato) is Agent Spike Devine, probably our best undercover operator. We will be your hosts as we sail to Bari, where extradition papers have been vetted and approved. We have secured a deluxe ocean-view suite for your use during the rest of the voyage, if you would care to use it."

She sat frozen in her chair. For long moments no one moved. Then she sighed deeply and turned her head away. A single tear slid across her ashen cheek. She was on her way home.

NEW OPPORTUNITIES

"Goddammit, Fergus, pay attention and quit fussing with that engine," demanded Frank, causing his brother to back away from the model electromagnetic locomotive planned for the new bullet train across the desert Midwest. Fred put down his fob on which he had been reviewing quarterly results. Frank was in his customary domineering mode.

"So, all right, the Parks Act didn't pass and it looks like we left a lot of money on the table. But we are Crouch Industries, and we don't get mad, we get even. I *will* sort out incompetents and take action. Meanwhile, I want you two bubbleheads to review some new opportunities that my staff has identified." Frank paused to assess his brothers' apparent interest. Frank paid attention. Fergus glanced at the model engine.

Frank flashed an image on an opaque window. In large print, it read simply "H_2O."

Puzzled, Fergus said, "Yeah, water. So what?" Fred simply looked intrigued.

"We're not going to be able to expand into the parks, but what I told you before still holds. Water will be king. Look what happened in the Midwest. Climate change and drought have caused water to be more valuable than gold. Sure, home reactors have knocked our liquid energy businesses on the ass, but reactor sales and replenishment programs are filling the gap. Now we plan to concentrate on water."

The image changed to a rendering of a huge factory complex surrounded by fifty-foot-high greenhouses. "Crouch Industries" was emblazoned above the industrial complex.

"Here's what Elever Snoddy and his team recommend," said Frank. "This is the ultimate combination of seawater, desalination, solar energy, and agriculture. Hell, saltwater covers seventy percent of our planet. With this technology we can guarantee, for a price, the elimination of future water shortages almost anywhere."

"Why are you bothering with solar? That's ancient technology. Reactors are the thing now," said Fergus, feeling superior. "They are **our** thing now."

This time, Frank did not ignore his younger brother. Exasperated, he said, "If you would stop playing with toys and antique television series for a few moments and listen to news, you would know there have been some rumblings about reactor 'fallout' lately—the escape of errant hydrogen protons that some people say make their hair and teeth fall out. Nonsense, of course, but Snoddy feels solar is a bit safer. Also, it integrates perfectly into the saltwater greenhouse system."

Chastened, Fergus made sidelong glances at the model greenhouses rotating before them, wishing he were back in his video museum. Fred, more studious, riffed through the sections of Snoddy's report on his fob. The projected financials impressed him. He addressed Frank.

"This is a nicely integrated system. I see that saltwater trickles through a membrane and evaporates as it meets hot air, making the greenhouse air cool and very humid. That moisture collects on the plants, helping them grow. And I like that cold sea water running through pipes causes condensation that is captured and used for irrigation. What did Snoddy call this? Elegant."

"Yes," said Frank, "and we can cause the desert to bloom. Food and water—at a price, of course. I think it is particularly clever how the integrated solar system outside turns water to steam that drives turbines generating electricity. That powers the desalination unit and the pumps. More fresh water. And the brine produced cools the solar system, making it more efficient."

"Too bad we can't set some of these up in the Midwest desert, help those people out," mused Fergus.

"If you looked at the report," said Frank, "you would see we have plans for the Great Salt Lake in Utah. Unfortunately, obnoxious environmentalists thwarted our plan of piping saltwater in from Hudson Bay or the Pacific coast. Turns out it wasn't economical anyway."

Fred agreed. "The famine problem seems to be going away with the great migration north to Canada. Manitoba is booming."

The business meeting continued as they focused on other aspects of their corporate operations. Loss of the national parks was a temporary setback. Golden business opportunities continued to arise.

Things were not going well for Sneath Naydir. His wife was divorcing him, citing in public documents his unnatural and carnal desires pertaining to phalanges. The divorce court ordered him to pay about eighty percent of his before-tax earnings to maintain his soon-to-be-ex-wife and children. Clients who paid handsomely for his assurances that they would be first in line to purchase a national park were firing him and his firm. His senior partner and good friend, Phylander Musti, was avoiding him, and no Susan in the firm would give him the time of day. His children preferred the company of their fobs to their father. He was on the verge of being clinically depressed. For solace, he purchased an anatomically correct model of a female foot from Amazons.com, but it was unsatisfactory.

He sat at his desk, trying to imagine Tureen O'Porto, auburn hair cascading around her face, bending over her foot, brushing shiny apple green polish on her dainty toenails just as his fob vibrated, announcing a call from the object of his desire.

There were no customary pleasantries.

"Sneath, how are things going?" she asked, already aware that he was an emotional and financial basket case.

"Well, you know, same old, same old," he said, pausing to consider his long relationship with Tureen, needing someone he could be forthright with, thinking "any port in a storm."

"Actually, Tureen, things are not so good either at home or on the job. And I have this pain in my stomach, too. Doctor says it's stress."

Out of habit, he added, "How about you?"

"I am doing OK, but I need to give you a heads-up. It's not good news."

Sneath, swallowing hard, reached into a top desk drawer and extracted the anatomically correct woman's foot model and stroked its outer edge. The dull sense of impending doom he experienced for the previous few days exploded into a trapezoid-shaped bundle of sharp pain, rising between his eyes and extending to the nape of his neck.

"Go on," he managed to say.

"Crouch Industries just gave our shop exclusivity on all its lobbying business with a major assignment to secure a monopoly on both coasts for their new saltwater agribusiness operations. I'm afraid they are cutting you out. I'm sorry, but what could we do but engage with them?"

"Yeah," he said ruefully, "that's been happening to me a lot lately. But, it's good to know what's coming. I expect they'll fire me by xmail. Thanks for letting me know."

"Sneath, there's more. It's about the late Ben Chang, whom I know you worked for in the past. Did he ever chew you out, express displeasure; get really pissed off at you? Be honest. It's important."

It had been a few years, but Sneath had an indelible recollection of Chang's last conversation with him.

"You could say that we did not part on friendly terms," he said. "He claimed I wasn't quick enough to obtain visas for his second wife's parents, who lived in Azerbaijan. They had been charged with arson, murder, and child molestation. Not an easy task, as you can imagine. There were harsh words and threats, and he refused to pay our final invoice. Why? What's it about?"

Tureen looked concerned.

"You remember how that little guy tried to attack me with acid? It was on all the local channels."

"Yes, I do. Bad business, right?"

"More than that," she said. "The little guy confirmed, as part of the allocution process at his trial, that Chang hired him to attack me. So, I'm calling everyone I know who did business with him to alert them to possible danger. For myself, I'm not sure that was the only person Chang hired to hurt me. I have been very careful, and you should be, too."

The pain between his eyes intensified, as did the tightness in his throat.

"Thank you for letting me know," he croaked, a raspy whisper.

Within hours, he offered his resignation to Phylander Musti, who accepted, packed up his private belongings in two bankers' boxes, and returned to the little apartment near DuPont Circle he shared with two goldfish.

That night he consumed vodka on the rocks, asked himself a thousand times how his life could have turned into offal so quickly, and cried. The next morning, he deposited the goldfish in front of a neighbor's door, placed his meager wardrobe in the trunk of a newly acquired Tesla roadster, pressed the silent ignition, and headed north.

In sunny Manitoba, some weeks later, Crouch Industries made a new hire. He was a middle-aged man with no special skills who passed the test for filter inspector at the company's newest saltwater agribusiness plant on the shore of Hudson Bay. His job was to examine the filter monitors on pipes sucking water from the bay, take the filter offline if he discovered obstructions, clean the filter, and return it to operation.

The most unpleasant part of the process was scraping away ocean debris. Many slimy and rotten things from the bay's depths, usually deadly white, misshapen, and foul smelling, lodged in the filters. No matter how hard he scrubbed, the odor never went away, making social life awkward and difficult.

As unpleasant as it was, Sneath was comfortable and relieved. Better than worrying about an attack by some crazed assassin hired by Benjamin Franklin Chang or suffering as an outcast in the capital, he thought.

The new virtual reality game NIRVANA!, which simulated space flight to the galaxy of Nirvana, incorporating the latest artificial "five"-sensory experience, was an overnight success. The game eliminated any politically correct restraints on actions or emotions, and players indulged their wildest space and futuristic fantasies at will. The game remembered a player's reactions to all past scenarios, learned favorite experiences, and created new game modes that generated maximum pleasure for the participant—without pernicious side or after effects. The players called themselves "Nirvies," and there were hundreds of millions of them.

The psychoactive substances industry suffered. Sellers of caffeine, alcohol, LSD, cannabis, cocaine, and other opioid painkillers saw remarkable sales decreases within weeks of the game's introduction. Merck, Novartis, Pfizer, and Bayer sued individually and collectively to halt sales of the game, but the International Court of Commerce justice denied their demands. Chief Legal Officer Barak Obama rejected the argument that the game was unpardonably addictive. His oft-quoted decision that the plaintiffs "were trying to stick their fingers, niggeldy piggeldy, into the hole in the dam with unclean hands" disallowed their claims, and NIRVANA! sales accelerated in response to the publicity generated by the Big Pharma suit.

Melvin Salmon, the game's creator, took his success in stride. The AEROTIVA game had made him a multimillionaire. Nine months after the introduction of NIRVANA!, important financial rating agencies estimated his personal worth at over nine billion new dollars. The shares he set aside for Portia, Tureen, and Agatha Johnson as a gesture of friendship and goodwill after the march against the Parks Act guaranteed each of them an immediate and luxurious retirement. He amused himself by imagining their reactions when he told them they had millions of new dollars at their disposal—tax free, of course, because Congress had discontinued the capital gains tax.

Melvin enjoyed the daily exercise of walking from his modest apartment to the cluttered office that he maintained on the ground floor of his research center, a refurbished transit terminal abandoned when Selfers® and magneto devices replaced public transport. Games research, marketing, and customer service groups had their workspaces on the building's periphery. Melvin's office was in the center of the complex, at the hub of his current passion, the special projects group.

Nucleon-driven linked computers stacked fifteen feet high filled half of the large open space Melvin saw from his office. The computers could sequence a complete human genome in less than a second and predict the results of genetic adjustments in the same period. From his fob, Melvin could identify defective genes and amino acid structures and quickly determine repair techniques.

Dr. Minny Patel, a chief assistant, handed him a tablet that showed results of the last twelve hours' calculations. "Boss, looks like we have confirmed the three factors that introduce autism to the embryo," she said as she projected the sequences on his screen.

"Did you see how long it takes the printer to fabricate the splice?" he asked.

"Piece a cake. We can have the program ready for submission to the NHGRI[6] this afternoon. I talked with Omar there, and he said they are eager to move on this. After all, they were pretty close to a cure for autism themselves just before Congress cut their funding."

Melvin agreed. Minny stood by as he reviewed hastily dictated notes on his fob.

"OK," he said, "Version 2.3 of the Down's syndrome cure software. Has that been verified?"

"Yes," she said, clicking her device. "It's scheduled for release early Tuesday. As you requested, this total freeware packet includes links to our serum warehouses and provides expedited delivery. The subscriber list is this long." She stretched out her arms to indicate a great number.

Melvin was eager to play with the two fobs and eleven monitors surrounding his desk, but Minny cleared her throat, indicating there was one more thing to discuss.

"That infant leukemia thing still is stumping our best people. We have not been able to identify the extraordinary factors that inhibit the application of palliative genome therapy that works on older children. The babies don't respond."

Melvin thought of Portia and what she told him about her childbirth experience when he called to congratulate her. He leaned back in his chair, chewed on a knuckle, and looked at a blank monitor screen.

"Did we sequence the babies' amniotic fluid?" he asked.

"No. Not yet."

"Give that a shot."

It proved to be the right shot.

Minny left. Melvin prepared himself for a meeting with his favorite group of thinkers—his "dingleberry" group. They were scientific researchers, writers, genetic engineers, artists, and journalists. He walked to the open conference room and took his place at the table.

"So, what do we need to do to save the world from itself today?" he asked.

---

6 National Human Genome Research Institute, formed in the early twenty-first century

SPAVINED GNATS

The *Washington Post* Society Section, in the drop-down labeled "Relationships," announced that Tureen Gwendolyn O'Porto and Lance Frederick Peppercorn were in a relationship.

The article described their backgrounds and the qualities and professions of their antecedents. Lance admitted to obtaining an English degree from Temple University and a master's degree in oceanography from Humboldt University in California. Tureen also learned that Lance's parents had been wealthy Midwest grain distributors operating many storage centers in Nebraska, Kansas, Iowa, and Missouri. The Great Drought forced them into bankruptcy. Their main income was a government farm subsidy for not selling their grain products. They lived in a trailer home in Missoula, Montana, and raised chickens. The information about Tureen's parents was similarly accurate.

The *Washington Post* prided itself on its in-depth reporting and mining scores of social networks for pertinent information.

Tureen persuaded Lance to leave his small apartment and move to her penthouse in Turnbury Tower with views of the Potomac River. Tureen found that being close to him morning and night intensified her ardor for this rugged outdoorsman. Their lovemaking was extraordinary. Like with fine Asian cuisine, they were hungry for more within an hour after feeling sated. Lance, who had numerous partners during the previous five years, was happily contented.

Tureen, suffering from a sexual dry spell for some time, and mildly unsure of her sexual orientation, was ecstatic. Lance validated her heterosexuality—passionately and frequently.

After a few months, however, they were both willing to enjoy conversations that did not culminate in thrashing about on the nearest horizontal surface.

They sat together on a settee facing the sunset on the veranda of her penthouse. Wine glasses in hand, they watched a fluorescent sun gliding toward the blue hills of the Appalachians, crowning the mountains with a golden haze. The slanting light set Tureen's ginger hair ablaze, and Lance reached to caress it, slowly pulling his fingers through thick tresses, making ringlets with his forefinger. A breath caught in her throat.

"Easy does it, buster," she said. "We're going to give Mister Master and the Princess of the Night a timeout. I really want my sleep tonight and don't need one thing to lead to another and show up at work yawning and red-eyed. The four governors from the western states are arriving to figure out how to persuade the administration to transfer the national parks in their states to them."

He relaxed his hand. "Like Arizona gets the Grand Canyon and Colorado gets the Rocky Mountain National Park?" There was a note of incredulity in his voice.

"Sure. Their support helped thwart the Parks Act. Since that battle is over and almost forgotten, they feel the time is right to pursue their plans to acquire the parks for themselves. It's been their goal all along."

"OK, I understand that. But, I'm troubled by your statement that the battle is over and forgotten. Christ, it was only two months ago. How could it be almost forgotten?"

"Well, this is Washington and, since there is general recognition that the parks matter is finalized, it's dead. And buried. Moving on to other things. Like the speaker of the House said the other day, 'Legislators have the attention span of a spavined gnat.' That's pretty short," she added.

"I'll have to take your word for it," said Lance. "But you were gung-ho to save the parks for everyone's use and fought hard to stop the act. Now you're telling me you will try to **give** the parks to western governors. There's something seriously wrong with this picture!"

Oh shit, she thought, he's going to appeal to my conscience. By now, she was convinced that she had one, and it was inconvenient. Ever since her glib answer that she was "unconscionable" to Portia's jibe, moral questions refused to be ignored. The conflicts between the demands of her work and the dictates of her conscience were painfully more pronounced. Moreover, here was her lover, her rugged outdoorsman, putting his finger on a very troubling aspect of her life. She did not answer. She raised her glass to filter the rays of the setting sun through its red liquid.

"I know it's hard to understand that sometimes I have to relax personal standards to make a living. It's called compromise," Tureen said.

"That's an expedient word for it, I suppose," said Lance, turning toward her on the settee. "In my experience, though, 'relaxing your standards' for money can be dangerous. I forget. How many pieces of silver did Judas get for turning on his boss?"

"That's not fair," she bridled. "It's just how we do business in the beltway."

The early chill of evening seeped between them, surrounded them, frosted their relationship.

"I think I'll turn in," said Lance. "Got an early meeting with the crew."

He left her on the settee, where she tried to ignore his taking leave and, hands on elbows, drew herself together, challenging the chill air, angry at Lance and his uncomplicated morality. She slept badly that night.

The governors and a phalanx of their aides crowded around the walnut conference table. Tureen rose to applause. The governors still glowed over their victory in defeating the Parks Act, and greedily anticipated Tureen's help in grasping spoils of combat—control of parks in their states.

"Thank you all for your superb support in helping your legislators in Washington recognize how wrong passing the Parks Act would be," she said. "I congratulate you on your efforts and services in keeping the national parks open to all our citizens."

From the governors rose a chorus of self-effacing comments and compliments for Tureen. The meeting was taking on the aspects of a lovefest.

"I don't know about you," she continued, "but when I work on a campaign I begin to internalize all the arguments I make to pursue my goal. By the time we came close to a vote, and after I experienced the Grand Canyon, I became absolutely convinced that maintaining federal control of the parks is critical. I even read essays by John Muir, who founded the Sierra Club, to discover his views. He convinced me that states, in the past, did a terrible job of managing these beautiful assets."

The members of her audience exchanged meaningful looks. Where was she heading with this dangerous talk?

"Unfortunately, I can't condone lobbying to undo the good work we all did to keep our parks free and open to all," she said. Disappointed and angry faces crowded around the table.

"If you will check your fobs, you'll see that we have listed highly qualified lobbying firms in the capital who will gladly take your money to try and remove the parks from federal control."

There were annoyed glances at the list of lobbying firms and muttered voices of disapproval. The governor of Arizona spoke up first.

"So, this is how you repay us?" she said. "You take our money, you earn our trust, and abandon us. Dammit, I authorized your visit to the Grand Canyon that my Arizonans paid for. If I'd a known how it would influence you, I'd a declared open season on redheads."

Similar sentiments cascaded around the table, but Tureen maintained her calm demeanor, smiling, though through clenched teeth. Finally, the conference room cleared as disgruntled politicians, vowing revenge, at best, and darker endings, at worst, filed away.

"That went well, I thought," said Tureen to her fob, turning it from the table to focus on herself.

"'Open season on redheads;' I thought that was a nice touch," said Agatha Jackson, who had monitored the meeting. "I appreciate your introducing the opposition. I don't want to underestimate them, but I think they can be persuaded to drop their claims to the parks. For example, I could threaten to reintroduce regulation of all the states' marijuana growers on federal lands."

"That would put a real dent in their budgets," said Tureen.

Just chatting with her friend and comrade in arms was a relief. Their conversation quickly turned to personal matters.

When she left her office that evening, eager to return to Lance, rain showers slicked the streets. Her Hummer waited half a block away, and she had to navigate among people with umbrellas and rain gear. A short man in a tan raincoat, clutching his hat, pushed toward her and passed on. She experienced a flash of bone-chilling fear and backed away, caught her breath, and moved quickly to her car.

How long will I be terrorized, she wondered, by the dead hand of that Chinese lecher?

Wylie and his wife, Linda, like many older couples, were uncomfortable using Selfers®. In spite of the Selfers®' laudable safety record, the wide expanse of nothing under their feet as they moved about the sky was scary. They arrived by taxi for their visit to Portia and Grover's home to meet Wylie's first great-grandson.

Linda, a former nurse, had answered many of the sleep-deprived couple's concerns during the past weeks. She reassured them that babies normally emit horrid, penetrating noises to attract attention. They were not bad parents because their baby cried.

Linda was as eager as Wylie to meet the newborn; it had been a long time since she cuddled an infant.

Baby Merson immediately clutched Wylie's little finger in a tightfisted grasp, seemingly smiling up at the fuzzy image of the person above.

"You forget how tiny and perfect they are," he told Portia, leaning in to caress the baby's soft head. "And how great they smell," added Linda, cradling the happy baby.

It was clear from further comments that there was no question that this baby was a paragon among all babies, destined to be a great leader, good looking and bright. Reassured by such effusive praise, the little one moved his bowels and began to drift off to sleep. Portia placed him in his Digicrib®, which cleaned and changed the baby, activated its audio and video alarm systems, and pressed the medium "lull" button. She gazed blissfully at her child as he slept.

They gathered around the kitchen table, drinking and waiting for a drone to deliver Asian takeout. Grover joined Wylie in a drink of scotch, Linda had sake, and Portia drank the dark beer recommended by her pediatrician to help her lactate. The room was warm and comfortable, its occupants familiar and contented.

"Wylie," said Grover, "Portia and I have decided on the name for our son."

"Yes," said Portia. "He will be called Peter Merson—no middle name. It is in honor of your friend, the senator, who died just before our son was born. It just seemed right that one door opened while another closed. His actual name, Pierre, didn't seem to fit, but we both can see a Pete Merson growing from that little bundle in there. I hope you like it."

Wylie put down his drink and tried unsuccessfully to contain the torrent of memories about his best friend, memories that made his eyes overflow. Linda took his hand.

"Yes," he said. "New life. Pete would appreciate that. And I'm sure he will be shedding his grace on his namesake. Wonderful, just wonderful."

Wylie regained his composure, smiled at the young couple, and raised his glass.

"I think I'll drink to that!" he said.

"Hey, girl, when do you think you'll be ready to come back to work?" asked Agatha Jackson.

Portia answered her fob during Tureen's third visit to see the baby. She projected their conversation to include Tureen.

"Maybe never. Motherhood is addicting, now that he almost sleeps through every night. And by the way, when does the new deputy director of the Interior Department think she'll have time for another visit here?" asked Portia.

"He's growing fast," said Tureen. "Be ready for college in a couple months."

The three friends continued their banter for a few minutes before Agatha repeated her question.

"I'm serious, Portia. And I don't mean returning to the National Green Defense League. I want you to work with me—as chief counsel for the agency. It's a big job with significant impact. I have direct hiring authority, and congressional approval is not required. I can't think of anyone better qualified for the position. No pressure, of course, but when could you begin?"

Portia smiled at her friend's pitch. She had given little thought to working again. Certainly, there was no financial need to do so. Grover's annual income from the family trust assured an easy, work-free life. Yet, the prospects of an important government position, of influencing the activities of a large agency, of making a difference were appealing.

Agatha correctly interpreted Portia's thinking.

She added, "You would be leading a group of dedicated people determined to enhance our natural heritage. It would be a great personal opportunity."

Agatha, seeing that Portia shifted her baby on her lap, then said, "There are significant government perks. Day care is included."

Portia and Tureen laughed at that naked attempt at coercion.

"We'll talk later," Portia said, seeing Peter Merson fidget, searching for a nipple. She turned off the fob and fed her greedy son, who aggressively gummed and sucked her breast. She felt wonderful.

MUIR

Agatha smiled as she concluded her conversation with Portia. She knew her friend was deliberate and determined, and that she would be foolish to refuse the opportunity offered. She might have to persuade her again but, in the end, she knew that Portia, with Tureen's encouragement, would join her to continue to battle against man's lesser angels. She asked her fob to remind her to call Portia again in a few days.

From a drawer in her desk she extracted a battered leather-covered notebook that she used in college. She flipped to the pages that contained her penciled notes on John Muir's writings, words that she reread from time to time. As the founder of the Sierra Club and a naturalist who played a major role in establishing the national parks his words seemed as appropriate and inspirational today as when they were written more than a century earlier.

She ran her finger down the page, and stopped to read.

"Any fool can destroy trees. They cannot run away; and if they could, they would still be destroyed—chased and hunted down as long as fun or a dollar could be got out of their bark hides, branching horns, or magnificent bole backbones. Few that fell trees plant them; nor would planting avail much towards getting back anything like the noble primeval forests.... It took more than three thousand years to make some of the trees in these Western woods—trees that are still standing in perfect strength and beauty, waving and singing in the

mighty forests of the Sierra. Through all the wonderful, eventful centuries...
God has cared for these trees, saved them from drought, disease, avalanches,
and a thousand straining, leveling tempests and floods; but he cannot save them
from fools..."[7]

"The battle we have fought, and are still fighting, for the forests is a part
of the eternal conflict between right and wrong, and we cannot expect to see
the end of it.... So we must count on watching and striving for these trees, and
should always be glad to find anything so surely good and noble to strive for."[8]

Trees and forests, she thought—a perfect metaphor for our national parks.
But, she sighed, there will always be fools.

The notebook went back into the desk. There was a long day ahead.

---

7 *Our National Parks* (1901), Chapter 10.

8 "The National Parks and Forest Reservations," in a speech by John Muir (Proceedings of the Meeting
of the Sierra Club Held November 23, 1895). Published in *Sierra Club Bulletin* (1896).